Praise for Unplugged

Most of us understand that our children need more nature in their lives. But the days of free-range childhoods have all but vanished, at least for the time being. So what's a busy parent to do? With *Unplugged*, Jason Sperling expertly presents perhaps the most powerful answer to this pressing question—family nature clubs. Dive in and revel in the insights. The result—nature connection—will be one of the most powerful gifts you will ever give to the children in your life.

Scott D. Sampson, author, How to Raise a Wild Child; host, Dinosaur Train; president & CEO, Science World

http://www.scottsampson.net

Most of us think our kids spend too much screen time. Most of us moan on Facebook about this problem. Here's a book to help BOTH generations rediscover the real world—and each other!

Lenore Skenazy, founder of the book, blog, and movement Free-Range Kids

http://www.freerangekids.com

I hope this inspiring book, *Unplugged*, moves far and wide and ignites a desire in people to find the wherewithal to start and spread their own family nature clubs, coalescing all in the movement to connect children, families, and communities to nature!

Janice Swaisgood, Director of Family Initiatives, Children & Nature Network

http://www.childrenandnature.org

Beyond creating a practical guide to forming and managing a successful, engaging nature program for families, Jason Sperling is an incredible storyteller that will inspire you to take your family, your friends, and your community out into nature. This book will become a staple of our Families in Nature recommended reading list.

Heather Kuhlken, Founder and Director, Families in Nature

http://www.familiesinnature.org

If we tell our kids to turn off the TV…then what? This book, that's what. A step-by-step guide to helping parents step out into nature and step back from the impossibly high demands of 21st century parenting, this book will help your family create memories that matter.

Ashley Trexler, Founder of LiesAboutParenting.com

http://www.liesaboutparenting.com

This step-by-step, easy-to-follow guide challenges you to unplug and reconnect with nature in a big way. Take the whole family and enjoy!

Mariana Ruiz, Author, Geekdad.com

http://www.geekdad.com

In the busyness of family life, quality time together is often in short supply. If you're ready to switch off from the distractions and on to making lots of cherished family memories, getting hands-on with nature and reconnecting with the people who mean the most to you, then this book is for you!

Tania Moloney, Founder of Nurture in Nature Australia

http://www.nurtureinnature.com.au

If you are a mother or father, then you already know what a minefield parenting can be. There is often a conflict between your gut instincts and what media and society is telling you that you ought to be doing. Here is a book that outlines a plan to help you be the parent that your intuition gently tells you to be. If you do only one thing as a parent, then help your child to connect with nature and adventure. Watching them do so will be the most fulfilling experience you can imagine. If you are nervous, let Jason lead you. You will be very glad that you did.

Wil Rickards, Outdoor & Adventure Educator, Where The Fruit Is

http://www.wherethefruitis.com

If you want to get your family outdoors more but lack guidance, this book is your roadmap. Not only will *Unplugged* get you from point A to point B—from a tech-inundated lifestyle to a nature-focused one offering quality family time—but Sperling also offers advice on best routes, potholes, and detours along the way. And he does it with heart.

Heather Mundt, Founder Momfari, freelance writer/editor

http://www.momfari.com

UNPLUGGED

15 Steps to Disconnect from Technology and Reconnect with Nature, Yourself, Friends, and Family

JASON RUNKEL SPERLING

Foreword by Kenny Ballentine

Afterword by Chiara D'Amore, Ph.D

FREE BONUS

As a thank you for buying my book, I have created a bonus area to help you on your *Unplugged* journey. The bonus area has a growing list of resources, including:

- Downloadable workbook

- Step-by-step creation guide

- Planning considerations

- Activity suggestions

- Tips for sustained success

- Planning worksheet

- Quick-start checklists

- Examples and templates

For access to the bonus area visit: www.jasonrunkelsperling.com/unplugged-resources

To my wife, Michele, and our children, Nyla and Silas, for welcoming our journeys with an adventuresome spirit and making our home the best place to return to!

CONTENTS

FOREWORD

There was a time when childhood was defined by unstructured time outside. It was a time when children were free to roam across fields, climb trees, explore creeks, and play ball in vacant lots. It was a time when children were not expected back in the house until the skies began to darken. When was this magical era? Actually, it was pretty much all of human history until about the last two decades.

We now live in a time where childhood is spent indoors. Today, the average American child spends 90 percent of his time indoors, and a whopping 6 to 10 hours per day in front of a screen! The developments of the past 20 years have combined to create a culture that is indoors and stationary. These developments include urbanization, massive advances in technology and digital media, the rapid disappearance of parks and other public green spaces, and a sharp increase in parental fear. Specifically, the fear of stranger danger, liability, and nature itself.

Why does this matter? When a kid is inside, they are virtually stationary, which is a major contributor to our current childhood obesity epidemic. Additionally, the medical community has now connected too much time inside with myopia and osteoporosis. Studies have also shown that children who live an indoor lifestyle are more likely to experience attention deficit disorder and depression.

What does nature have to offer? In short, it promises happier, healthier, and smarter kids! There is an ever-growing body of research suggesting that academic performance goes up as time outside in nature is increased. Playing outside encourages creativity, problem solving, and teamwork. It also promotes introspection and provides kids with a peaceful and quiet space in an otherwise noisy and frenzied world. Time outside fosters a reverence for nature and a sense of stewardship for the planet. And finally, let's not forget that playing outside is fun! It deeply saddens me to think that so many kids are completely unaware of what they are missing.

What can be done about it? The first and most powerful thing you can do is to take a child outside today. Take kids out into the garden and have them get their hands dirty. Turn over rocks and look for bugs. Walk barefoot on the grass. Go for a hike. There are countless ways that you can get kids engaged with nature. Often, the only thing that a child needs to get started is a caring parent, teacher, or mentor who can show them what the outdoors has to offer.

The book you are holding in your hands is an invaluable resource for connecting children, families, and communities to the wonders of the natural world. Jason Sperling masterfully combines his wisdom with heartwarming true life stories and just a hint of nostalgia. The tools and advice in this book will empower you to engage in a more authentic connection with nature, improve family relationships, and build resilient communities. So, lace up your boots, step out your door, and take a deep breath. This will be a journey to remember!

Kenny Ballentine

Director of the documentary film "Nature Kids", host of the "Nature Kids Radio" podcast and founder of The Nature Kids Institute

ACKNOWLEDGMENTS

I would like to thank the members of my family and the families of our family nature club—Running Wild—who participated in our outings, rain or shine, mud or snow, and inspired this book that allowed me to share memories and photos of our experiences.

A special note of thanks to Richard Louv, author of *Last Child in the Woods* and co-founder of the Children & Nature Network; Janice Swaisgood, director of the Children & Nature Network's Natural Families initiative; and Chiara D'Amore for their contributions to my inspiration and knowledge.

INTRODUCTION

Nyla rides a fallen evergreen tree with other children on a multi-family camping trip in Roosevelt National Forest.

6:30 AM. I'm on my second cup of coffee, and my daughter, Nyla, age 3, has wandered beyond our tiny kitchen area to join the other children who have all finished breakfast and are now exploring the forest that surrounds our camp. They caper in and out of view and settle on a fallen evergreen tree. The tree's girth is a challenge at first, but Nyla scrambles up to sit between two other children. It's a crisp morning, chilly enough for winter hats and coats, yet still the children are lit up with joy—they are free, unencumbered by adult agendas, schedules, and fences of urban living. Out here in nature, they flex their independence and discover what so many other children have found outside—serenity and solace.

Throughout our two-night multi-family camping trip, I observe Nyla grow in so many ways. She helps me prepare breakfast and then later carry our inflatable kayak, life jackets, and supplies down to the mountain reservoir hundreds of yards away. We paddle across miles of waters, sun ourselves and leap from rocks with the other families, and share memories and stories by campfire light. The hours seem to span days, and she is ever-present, glued to the expansive vistas, community interactions, and family bonds. Her happiness is marked with an absence of the complaining and whining typical of toddlers— instead, replaced by an eagerness to take on responsibility, and a level of engagement that is far rarer when at home.

My memories of growing up in Colorado abound with experiences in nature. We hiked, we backpacked, we rafted, and we skied. We played in streams, mountains, and oceans (not in Colorado, obviously!). Until becoming a parent myself, I never realized how much of those childhood experiences were made possible by my parents' interest and participation in ensuring that I spent a great amount of time outdoors. When I was young, this was facilitated by living in the mountains and my parents' own values, which allowed for unstructured time and play outdoors. Then it was Cub Scouts, Boy Scouts, and travel that took me deep into nature on a regular basis, often with peers, and facilitated greatly by my parents' participation and leadership. This camping trip, several years ago, revealed the role that I would need to play if I wanted to raise my children in a similar way—connected to nature.

Shortly thereafter, I was introduced to the concept of family nature clubs in Richard Louv's *Last Child in the Woods*. I learned about nature deficit disorder and unstructured nature play, and discovered that my uneasy feelings about modern childhood were a reflection of the massive shift in the reality children face today. Children now spend less time in nature than in any previous generation. Their connection with the natural world is being lost, and at the same time we are facing an increase in obesity, physical maladies, and disconnected communities. Companies have mastered the art of selling indoor, screen-based products that diminish children's outdoor, unstructured nature-play—play that enhances their development and connection. The future leaders—our children—need our help now.

Why I Started a Family Nature Club

I never imagined myself as someone who would organize outdoor events for groups of families. But I desperately wanted a solution for my children to ensure they enjoyed a childhood as rich with nature experiences as I had.

I desperately wanted:

- More unstructured outdoor play, and for my children to enjoy independence and interact with nature devoid of adult agendas, following their own whims—not just by putting them in a day- or week-long program, and not a short after-school program either. I wanted to give them long stretches of time on a frequent basis. Even with activities that are more adult-guided, I wanted to ensure they were complemented with intentional space and time for unstructured outdoor play.

- Experiences in which our whole family could participate with friends and parents, regardless if I had a daughter or a son. While Boy Scouts worked well for my brother and me, my desire was to find activities that would allow my children and family to enjoy those experiences together, and not put the children in separate gender-based groups (such as the Boy Scouts is in the U.S.) where parents were not participants.

- Deep interaction with nature—not experiences in urban, manicured settings or those that maintained a distance from nature and viewed it like a museum exhibit. I wanted to get my children into the wilds and wilderness so that they could touch, see, smell, and develop a lifelong bond with nature like I had.

- Something that was easy to coordinate with a consistent community, rather than a series of one-off play dates where a cancellation could ruin the plan, or result in me spending hours and hours researching and registering for a variety of programs that would put my children into one new community after another.

What I wanted was an easy way to organize an epic group of families eager to adventure with us all the time!

The family nature club concept is an evidence-based proven solution to these and more challenges faced in modern childhood. Quite simply, it is "a group of people interested in connecting children with nature on a regular basis for nature-centered experiences to instill wonder and engendered curiosity."—Richard Louv

The idea of starting my own club for my daughter filled me with excitement. But we also had a newborn son...so I chose not to act. I finished the book and tucked it away.

The book sat on my side table for a couple years. Then, it happened.

In the spring of 2015, my family and I decided we were ready to try building a family nature club. My children were then five and two, and needed much more outdoor time with friends. As much as I didn't want to give up my solitary claim on our family activities, I knew it was time. We began our club with a good dose of hesitation and apprehension, organizing just a few friends and infrequent multi-family events in nature. Over the last year we have slowly and gently grown the club, inviting new folks as the children joined new classrooms and communities. Today, I plan weekly events for our club, and have events that have drawn dozens of families. Our family nature club brings immense joy to our children and family. It's building a community I never would have imagined being a part of, and giving our children an experience in nature that is profoundly fun and both developmentally and educationally valuable. Others across the world echo almost the exact same sentiment and results for their children and family when participating in such clubs.

The concept of a family nature club is easy to understand and implement. It is flexible and powerful. It crosses gender, race, and socio-economic barriers—truly a community-building device. It forges a lifelong bond between people and nature—our home and mother, and what sustains our presence here. As I discovered this potency, I began to wonder why more people are not aware of the family nature club concept. Why, if the concept has been around by name since 2006, and previously in effect for decades, is it not mainstream and known everywhere?

This Book Is Powerful

The life I have created from following the ideas and practices I share is purely amazing. I see it in the eyes and smiles of my own children and family. I have received accolades in person and through the grapevine about the experiences my community has created from what I share in this book. People frequently come up to me and say, "You are a rock star!" Well, no I'm not, but the concept of family nature clubs is!

I stand behind every one of the steps you will learn here—I have experienced the success of them firsthand, and there is mounting evidence of their effectiveness.

Unplugged is the culmination of what I have learned in over four decades of personal experiences and skill mastery in nature, becoming an experienced outdoorsman, and now running my own family nature club. I don't just talk the walk—I walk the walk. And with this book, you can too.

Why Did I Write This Book?

This book is an effort to increase the awareness of family nature clubs. It's stunning that more people haven't heard about them.

The goal is to inspire you to move into action! The focus of the following pages present short vignettes of our experiences intertwined with the simple steps you can take to build your own family nature club.

Reach for Your Dreams

If you're like me, when you became a parent it was like walking into a foreign land with little to guide you. Hopefully, you began your parenting journey with high hopes for the life you'd craft for your children and family. But then, all of a sudden, you have a baby to take care of . . . and after that a toddler. It's a challenging, overwhelming time . . . and as you slowly emerge from the sleepless nights and start to orient to this new landscape, you just might remember the dreams and wishes you have for your children. Finding the right balance between work, your relationships, and your family is challenging. Being a good parent is hard, and being a great parent is absolutely harder.

With good intentions, persistence, and commitment, you can achieve your greatest dreams. My hope is that this book will give you a valuable tool for your journey and help you take those intimidating first steps. I promise you this:

If you read this book and follow the steps, your life will be greatly transformed!

ABOUT THIS BOOK

"What if parents, grandparents, and kids around the country were to band together to create nature clubs for families? What if this new form of social/nature networking were to spread as quickly as book clubs and Neighborhood Watches did in recent decades? We would be well on our way to true cultural change."

—Richard Louv, author of *Last Child in the Woods: Saving Our Children from Nature-Deficit Disorder*, and chairman emeritus, Children & Nature Network

Getting unplugged is impossible without passion, enthusiasm, gusto, inspiration, and the deep rewards that come with doing something magnificent.

It's easy to get stuck in a rut while following the status quo—overscheduling children with adult-guided or screen-based activities that are meant to enrich their future. The results of this are long unwelcomed days for your children where you become a shuttle service getting them from one activity to the next. By the end of each day, your whole family is exhausted and spent from trying to do so much.

This book shows you how to unplug. By following a proven and flexible approach to building a family nature club, you will be inspired. You will find yourself restored and energized, and your family rejuvenated.

Here is a brief look at what each chapter in this book will cover.

Chapter One, "Law of Attraction," will show you how to define a purpose, plan, and pick a name for your family nature club. This is the foundation upon which the rest of your work is built, and is really fun once you see how easy it is!

Chapter Two, "Build Your Tribe," highlights simple and non-confronting ways to find and solicit initial members for your family nature club. This approach works especially well for anyone who is hesitant and unsure of what kind of response they will get and commitment they can make.

Chapter Three, "Circle of Influence," focuses on how to get ideas for events. It includes how to approach the people you already know to get ideas, and shares a lot of ideas and research methods to uncover even more ideas!

Chapter Four, "Victim vs. Leader Perspective," helps you understand one of the most important roles of the leader—how to scout and research locations for events in advance and document what is important to ensure a hassle-free and fun time for everyone. This chapter also helps you understand how rewarding it can be to have the responsibility of scouting locations.

Chapter Five, "FLY," emphasizes the steps in writing event descriptions for family nature club outings that will inspire, attract, and motivate participants while avoiding any confusion or potential problems. The steps are accompanied by examples so you can quickly see the format in context.

Chapter Six, "Power of Efficiency," shows you how to use technology to efficiently organize the logistics of events and communications with your group. A number of different solutions and strategies in choosing technology that is the right fit for your time, skills, and family nature club are discussed

Chapter Seven "Disconnect," helps you become a good host at family nature club events by reviewing core practices for being present and guiding your families, versus sitting back and tapping away on your smartphone. This chapter also introduces some fundamentals for gently leading your group in a way that results in positive responses.

Chapter Eight, "Stay Safe," shows you how to navigate the issues surrounding liability so you're confident to start your family nature club from a legal perspective.

Chapter Nine, "Attachment and Desire," focuses on how to let go of being in control and having goal-oriented activities, giving children independence and allowing events to be child-led. If you are like many parents striving to give children the best possible opportunities in life, this will be an important one for you.

Chapter Ten, "Love," teaches you how to manage family nature club events when you have low attendance at your event. Your response will greatly determine the quality and future of your club. A heart-centered approach is combined with smart marketing strategies.

Chapter Eleven, "Small Wins," walks you through how to promote your family nature club and raise attendance through content creation, even when you are just starting out and don't have a lot to work with.

Chapter Twelve, "Listen   to   Truth," emphasizes the importance of collecting feedback from members, and how to use their input to guide future events. This includes navigating both positive and negative feedback to the benefit of the club.

Chapter Thirteen, "Audacious Dreams," shows you how to start with the skills you have and then slowly build your capabilities and the scope of your family nature club one step at a time until you reach your big dreams. This chapter introduces a framework that will help you focus on the highest priority actions to get your children and family into nature as quickly as possible, and continually refine what your role is and how advanced and complex your events become.

Chapter Fourteen, "Discover A Wise Sage," provides a step-by-step process for adding educational aspects to your events without having to learn anything yourself. The chapter explores a variety of methods and resources for getting a third-party expert involved with your club events.

Chapter Fifteen, "Delegate Your Fears and Worries," focuses on how to find and network with other leaders of family nature clubs, so you don't have to reinvent the wheel but instead can work on making the wheel more aerodynamic. There is a vibrant community of other like-minded folks who are eager to help you and resolve concerns you have based on their own experiences.

Each chapter also includes my personal picks, and the exact steps I took to develop my club into what it is today. At the end of the book are useful resources (worksheets, tip sheets, forms, samples, templates, and other materials) that will give you guidance and make it easier for you to get going and take that first step!

Let's begin.

CHAPTER 1

LAW OF ATTRACTION

Silas discovers a complex of brush and trees. His excitement is contagious, and he is shortly joined by other children.

10 AM. Silas has abandoned his down jacket and balances precariously as he makes his way across a fallen tree. Nearby children observe his wide smiles and hear his shrieks of glee when he navigates gravity with each step. Several children

make their way to balance along the sprawling series of fallen trees, forming a chain of youngsters and marching like a scene out of a dreamy fairy picture book. The sun beams down on them and draws their attention to the flock of geese that pod by giant ghost-like Russian olive trees. The children themselves move like a pack, leaping off the log and then stringing between ponds gurgling with frogs and trees peppered with birds. We are just minutes away from our city, but the children have discovered a perfect piece of nature.

Soon the heat awakens anthills that bloom with flurries of activity. Ants scurry out from and across their hills and nearby ground, mesmerizing the pack of children. A smaller group of children drop down and sit there, next to the miniature workers, and dig into their snacks. Other children notice the food and water being consumed, and they too come to sit and begin to eat and drink. The sun radiates, as do the children's smiles. They are together, they are happy, and their joy is contagious to the parents who watch from nearby.

The Law of Attraction—"like attracts like"—is a powerful mechanism. It's easy to see it in action with children's play. It's also a useful concept when thinking about starting your own family nature club. With just a few steps, you can use the Law of Attraction to help you unplug by attracting other people to what you are doing. It all starts by defining your idea!

Crafting a Purpose, Plan, and Name for Your Family Nature Club

I didn't fancy myself an organizer, and when I got up the courage to try it, I encountered self-doubt and resistance. Having seen the powerful Law of Attraction in effect throughout my life, the first step I decided to take was to put my idea out into the universe. My hope was that it would draw others who wanted something similar in their lives. And it did! To harness the Law of Attraction for your family nature club, there are two steps you must take: come up with a purpose and plan, and then come up with a name for your club.

Family Nature Club Purpose and Plan

Family nature clubs come in many different shapes and colors. By clearly articulating the five Ws of information gathering, you can quickly come up with the purpose and plan for your club. Once you've answered the five Ws, you'll have made a lot of the big decisions that will guide your scheduling, marketing, what types of activities your club will do, and more.

The five Ws are who, what, where, when, and why.

Who will be the members of your club? Will it be open to the general public, or a group for your church, school, nonprofit, or other organization?

What will you do? Will you focus on unstructured nature play, adult-led activities like skill building and naturalist education, or outdoor activities like hiking, boating, camping, etc.? Or will it be some combination?

Where will your events take place? Will you be at different locations close to where you live, go on long trips, or always go to the same location? Will it vary? You can plan to start one way and be open to evolving things as you go!

When will your events take place? Will events be organized once a month, once a week, or several times a week? Will they be during the week, weekends, day, or nighttime? How long will they be? A couple of hours, a half day, overnight events, etc. Scheduling events at a consistent time and in advance will help families get them on their calendar.

Why are you excited about the family nature club? Is it because of a personal reason, because of the research backing the value of nature-based experiences, or because you want to build a community? It may be all of these. There are resources you can use to bolster your knowledge to help you communicate to your families why this is important.

Don't worry if you don't have all of the answers here. Through this book, you'll learn a lot that may shape your thinking. Once you have thought this through a bit, it's a good idea to write it down. Initially, you can write your purpose and plan quickly, and come back to it later if you want to write it more eloquently. For now, just get it down in a rough format so you know the reasoning behind what you are doing. Having a clearly articulated purpose and plan that you share with others will draw interested families when you put it out there. It will feel a bit like magic. It's the Law of Attraction at work!

Family Nature Club Name

Once you've solidified your purpose—and remember, this can always evolve—it's time to come up with your name. This is my favorite part! Having a name is necessary to help you with your future communications. You'll use your name when you communicate with your club, for example in your marketing materials such as a website, email, or flyers.

You are a big part of what drives the name of your club, as well as what the club's *purpose* is. If you're creating a club for a nonprofit or other existing group, you may want to include that name in your club name. If you're creating a public group for a specific location, such as a city, you may want to include that in the name of your club. If the club is for you and some friends, you may not need any existing name, and you can be creative and come up with something that is more personal to you. In any case, the name should be something you LOVE, and something that fits your personality and the personality and values you wish to manifest for your club.

Jason's Picks

Here is my initial purpose, written out:

A small private club for families at the school my children attend (the who) interested in connecting children with nature for unstructured nature play and adult-guided activities (the what). The events will take place close to Boulder (where I live) and sometimes venture into the mountains (the where). The events will be organized regularly weekly or twice monthly (the when).

The goals of the group are to increase the opportunity children have in nature, to have fun, to provide active screen-free experiences, to forge a deep lifelong relationship and skills in nature, and to build a community that can grow with our children (the why).

Notice that it answers the five Ws and, while not as specific as it could be, makes up the plan for my club (at least when I first started it).

The name I chose for my club is Running Wild. Running Wild was an idea my wife had that came up in our informal brainstorming session at the breakfast table one day. We talked about several different ideas, but this is the one that resonated the most. I wanted something short that wasn't tied to a specific organization or location, but rather emphasized my desire for an active adventurous childhood for my kids.

With a purpose, plan, and name, I started telling people about what I was doing, and others grew excited! This is the Law of Attraction in full effect!

What You've Learned

In this chapter, you've learned how the Law of Attraction can help you start your family nature club. You've learned how to come up with a purpose, plan, and name for your club.

CHAPTER 2

BUILD YOUR TRIBE

The children—muddy, dripping wet, cold—stand near the rushing creek foraging for wild things in the rainy morning.

9:22 AM. Everything is soaking. Just absolutely soaking. Silas slops about on the muddy bank and then stands to watch his sister, Nyla, as she steps onto a slippery stump. It's shoulder season in Colorado, and we're not quite dressed for the unexpected temperatures. Nor did all of us come prepared with backup clothes for kids who dare, against the weather, to get soaked feet and legs. At first it's just a few families. We assume others are taking a rain check on this outing, and we try to keep our spirits high as our bodies slowly get colder and colder.

A few steps later, one after another, the children step into the frigid current. Like hummingbirds, we swoop in and pull the children back onto land. Not every child's feet are wet, but those with shorter boots are uncomfortable and try to fight back tears. We quickly start the process of taking off wet socks and putting on dry ones. For those less prepared parents, spare socks are borrowed from other families. Tears are replaced with smiles, and relief gives way to curiosity. As the play resumes, other families slowly arrive, and soon we have a gaggle of children mucking about the creek again, kids being kids.

Building your family nature club tribe—even when you are starting at the very beginning, without a tribe—is easy once you get started! It is also incredibly rewarding for you, your children, your family, and your community. Like any community building, you just need to start the recruiting process.

How to Solicit Members for Your Family Nature Club

How you go about finding and soliciting members for your family nature club depends on what kind of group you want to create.

You can start small and privately (with just a few close friends), or you can launch very publicly, soliciting families in your neighborhood, at your children's school, at community organizations like scouts, or at other organized groups.

There's a variety of easy ways to reach out to folks.

Email is an efficient communication tool because it allows you to directly contact individuals in bulk. Plus, people tend to open and read emails, especially if they are from someone they know. If you are organizing your club for an existing group (like a nonprofit, school, church, or other group), there may be an existing email list that you can request to make your job easier. There are many free emailing services that you can use to allow you to easily email many people at one time.

Phone (and email) will allow you to contact a variety of other groups, such as local recreation organizations and stores (that frequently have message boards), other youth groups, outdoor enthusiast groups, church groups, and more. Spreading the word this way may take time, but once you've built connections with the leaders of these groups, your message will be distributed to a wide and engaged audience.

In person communication is very effective by nature. For groups you are already a part of, you can make an effort to talk to people when you see them on a regular basis. It can either be one-on-one or you can schedule a time to make an announcement as part of a larger group gathering. You can also reach out to existing groups that you are not a part of and find out if they'd allow you to drop by to make an announcement. You can start by talking with your existing friends, families in the neighborhood, and co-workers who have children.

Newsletters, newspapers, or other publications are similar to email in that you can reach a broad audience with one announcement. Whether you choose a traditional media like newspapers or reach out to websites and blogs that focus on your local community really depends on your goals and the audience of the publication. This can be a very useful way to attract people who share your interests that you don't know yet. You'll need to first contact the editor of the publication to find out their submission requirements, and then provide a short description of your club and how to get involved.

Marketing materials like flyers and websites take a bit of extra work, but nowadays there are a variety of free or nearly free tools to assist your design efforts. You can post flyers at schools, libraries, community recreation centers, and other group facilities. You can set up public groups on social networks. By adding keywords and images that relate to your club, you may quickly attract local families.

For example, I initially set up my club using Meetup.com, and within just a couple of days had over 40 families join the group! If you create a standalone website and add relevant content (such as frequent blogging), search engines will index your website and people will find you through their searches. Flyers can be created, printed, and posted at different places throughout your community, such as your child's school, local gyms, and aftercare message boards. You'll just need to go to the front desk and explain what you are doing.

Word of mouth tends to happen on its own—if you build a good club!—and helps attract new members to your club.

Jason's Picks

Since I wasn't sure the level of sustained commitment I could make and exactly how much effort organizing an ongoing club would take, I decided to start very simply. I wrote up an email introducing the name of my club and its purpose, and asked a few friends if they'd be interested in joining. The friends I sent the email to were all families of children in my daughter's school. While I emailed less than a dozen folks, the response I received was overwhelmingly positive.

Here is my original email:

> Subject: Interested in joining a family nature club?
>
> Dear friends,
>
> I've been really interested in starting an outdoor adventure group with local families. Below are some details. If you're interested, please let me know. There is also an important question at the end. I'd love your input. Thank you!

The tentative name of the group is Running Wild family nature club. It is modeled after the family nature club idea introduced in Richard Louv's book_*Last Child in the Woods* and promoted through the Children & Nature Network. You may have heard of *Last Child in the Woods* at our school. Much of the research and suggestions that Louv discusses in his book parallel the philosophy of Waldorf and the ideals of families raising children in this area. If you're interested, this page has a VIDEO and more details about the Louv's family nature club concept:

www.childrenandnature.org/movement/n aturalfamilies/

The basic idea behind Running Wild family nature club is to get a group of people interested in connecting children with nature together on a regular basis for "nature-centered experiences to instill wonder and engendered curiosity." These could take the shape of unstructured nature play (go to a location and let the kids explore), and sometimes these could take the shape of adult-guided activities (a hike, mountain biking, etc.). My intention is to find places close to Boulder, such as open space, trails, greenbelts, and pockets of wilderness—and sometimes venture into the mountains.

This isn't like a playgroup, play date, or day camp. We'll be outside with an interest in re-creating the type of nature experiences and free play that occurred more naturally and frequently in our childhood, and our parents' childhood. There will not be strict rules. For example, the group does not always have to stay together if a number of children wish to go off in a different direction. During unstructured nature play, the goal will be to step away and allow the children to interact without parent involvement, and without an agenda or set of goals besides "being there." Of course, this will vary as our activities vary, and so a group hike or camping trip will be structured differently. In any case, children will not be dropped off and left. Parents will need to be with their children, and will be responsible for them. This is something that both parents could attend, or one parent, or you can alternate. There are not any age restrictions or fees.

I can see that a group like this could grow with our children, and as the teenage years arrive so too may our activities change. I grew up rafting, skiing, and snow caving in the winters, and hiking and camping all year 'round. While Boy Scouts played a big role in my life back then, I'm curious about creating a group that both my daughter and son could be a part of together.

If you're interested, I'd love to find out what type of meeting time would work best for you and your family. If you're not interested, no worries.

***

I sent this out before planning any events or setting anything up for my club because I wanted to make sure I could get people to join the club. However, many clubs start in a different order, such as creating all of their marketing materials and planning the first few events, or a whole calendar year of events, and then starting to solicit members. It really depends on the purpose and plan of your club. Your ability to solicit new members for your club also varies on your location. Larger urban areas will be easier to get new members because of the size of the population and the pool of families that you can approach. If you're unsure, like I was, whether or not you will be able to attract members, one easy way you can test this out is by creating a trial account on Meetup.com and seeing if, by announcing your club there without any marketing, you attract signups. You may find that within just a few days you'll have dozens of families sign up!

What You've Learned

In this chapter, you've learned how to build your tribe for your family nature club, and how to find and solicit members for your club.

CHAPTER 3

CIRCLE OF INFLUENCE

The pack of children avoids the stairs and pushes their heavy mountain bikes up the hill towards the Corkscrew.

10:35 AM. Sunrays beam down on the grassy slope as children trek upwards towards the mesa at the sprawling Valmont Bike Park. Dirt beneath nails, sweat-covered brows, muscles aching; each child is inspired by the hive mentality and positive social pressure. At the top of the mesa they turn east and peddle their hearts out to the top of the ominous Corkscrew Trail—a series of switchbacks that edge down a steep face of hard-packed, rutted singletrack.

Many of the children have been here before. Until now, few have had the gusto to launch downward with sufficient momentum to avoid crashing and acquiring bloody knees and hands. The older boys explode into the Corkscrew first. The others follow. My daughter watches, clenching her fear back. I'm filled with trepidation too. The Corkscrew has notoriously ended several of our past visits to the park, always when my daughter goes too slow and, without enough momentum, wipes out on the very first turn. But this time is different: I watch as she draws courage—fearlessness—from her friends and pedals fiercely down and into the curve. Her tires rattle across the packed dirt, then upward, and she cranks her steering into a brilliant arc. She makes it! I'm relieved. She shrieks with joy, her sounds echoing amidst the cacophony of joyous celebration from the pack. It's a beautiful moment, and I'm grateful for having had other parents suggest we visit Valmont Bike Park with the club.

The circle of influence is the idea of being proactive about things we can do something about, and not being stuck in inaction because of what we cannot control. Getting ideas of what kind of events to plan for your family nature club can feel overwhelming at first, especially if you're just getting started. However, if you focus on what you can control—your circle of influence—you will discover that you have a lot of resources that will help you plan events that foster profound experiences, and that becomes a huge motivator.

How to Get Ideas for Your Family Nature Club

As with the other steps in building your family nature club, the types of events that resonate with you and your group will depend on your purpose. Your location and community will also impact your options.

Some basic ideas for outings include:

- Unstructured nature play

- Nature walk/hiking

- Star gazing

- Car camping

- Backpacking

- Boating

- Surfing

- Mountain biking

- Skiing

- Snow shoeing

- Nature programs

- Naturalist education

- Primitive skills education

- Birding

- Bird banding

- Volunteering with local forestry groups

- Volunteering with local farms

These may seem vague to the newcomer. To get inspired, you'll want to do a little research on your local area, how the experience for your club will change based on the season, and what other groups are doing in the outdoors. Crafting events that are appropriate for the season is especially important. For example, visiting farms during spring, boating and exploring creeks in the summer, snow play and learning about hibernation in the winter, etc. The research can be fun and rewarding (and you don't need to do it all at once). I've found that a combination of approaches works best, and these can evolve over time.

As the leader of your group, when you are doing research, you need to be mindful about checking in with all property owners about any requirements for bringing groups onto their land. Some property owners don't have any requirements, some just want a basic heads up, and some require liability insurance. It varies widely depending on who owns the land and the type and size of your group.

Here are some ways to research ideas:

Feedback from your members is a great way to get ideas. Parents will often have their own experiences and desires for what they want to do. You can ask for feedback from your members casually at events, by asking open-ended questions by email or on your website, or by talking with them outside of outings. What's great about planning events based on feedback is that you know at least some of your members will be very excited to join the event. I've learned about a lot of lesser-known locations from members that have turned into incredible experiences. Some clubs will use Survey Monkey for getting feedback—it is free up to 10 questions and 100 responses. You can include a link to your survey in a thank you follow-up email after each event.

Asking local public officials is really effective, and also helps uncover new ideas. Officials at your city, county, Forest Service, Bureau of Land Management, National Parks, conservation and outdoor education nonprofits, and other organizations are very welcoming to inquiries. Many of them are paid as public officers, and part of their jobs is to help support groups like family nature clubs understand and access land. They can provide specific ideas for places to go and activities to do, and point you in the direction of free materials that are available. You can connect with these folks by email, phone, and in person. I've had correspondence with folks at every one of these types of organizations, and have been pleasantly surprised at how much help they provide!

Online research is a great place to start, and can be a wonderful supplement to getting feedback from members and inquiring local public officials. There are almost an unlimited number of websites that document in great detail locations, trip ideas, parks, and more. This is an especially good way to discover opportunities for educators, naturalists, and other special guests to speak to or guide your group. From websites, blogs, and social networks you can discover a wealth of ideas for your local area. Besides getting ideas, online research is great at providing content (such as text, images, directions, tips, and more) that you'll be able to use in the descriptions of your events. I do online research for every one of my events, and find it extremely efficient and useful.

Other nature clubs are a great way to get inspired. There is a national listing of family nature clubs that you can use to find some in your area, and many use Meetup.com to find and solicit members, providing a great listing of past successful events. In essence, other nature clubs are trailblazing for you—they frequently will have already done much of the research that you otherwise would need to start from scratch. For example, the family nature club in my area had scheduled events with a local farm as well as an organization offering primitive skills education, both which seemed like perfect fits for my group. So I copied their ideas and planned a couple of events just like theirs!

Networking with local naturalists takes longer, but results in big rewards. It takes time to find and build relationships with outdoor specialists in your area, but once you've connected with them, they are perfect for advising on ideas of how to get families out into nature. They also frequently are open to helping you find and solicit members for your group, as it aligns with their goals of getting more people involved with what they love. By talking to friends and families in your club, you will naturally start to spread awareness of what you are doing, and this will result in introductions you otherwise may not have had. I've found and have been introduced to several local naturalists, and my relationships with them have been very valuable for getting new ideas for our club.

Keeping track:

Start a working document with a list of all of your ideas. Some ideas you may be ready to schedule, while others may require extra discovery and planning, such as setting up an event that is led by a naturalist from your city parks division. Try to start thinking about the sequence of events over the course of the next few weeks, months, or even an entire year.

Jason's Picks

I use all research methods! I love getting feedback from my members the best, and find doing so in person gets the best response. However, in the beginning (before I had any members), I found researching online and reaching out to local public officials to be the most effective. Both approaches are easily accessible, highly responsive, and relevant for my local area.

What You've Learned

In this chapter, you've learned how to find ideas for your family nature club. You've learned some basic ideas, and where and how to research and get inspired about these ideas.

CHAPTER 4

VICTIM VS. LEADER PERSPECTIVE

Nyla and Silas plunge into the creek that runs alongside the trail we were scouting. Seconds after I took this photo, they were soaked!

10:50 AM. After departing a nearby wildlife preserve featuring over a dozen ponds, we arrive at our second location to scout for our family nature club. This location features a trail that runs along a shallow creek, weaving through woodlands teeming with waterfowl. The trail was recommended to me by a naturalist with the Open Space and Mountain Parks department, specifically for its designed access to the water. Children are always attracted to water, so I thought we should check it out.

About a hundred yards up the trail we come upon the first water access point. The sun and warming temperatures invite the children to take off their shoes and immediately enter the water. Nyla wades from a tiny beach towards a boulder. Moments later, Silas, still only two years old, follows as best he can, but they quickly come upon a deeper pool. Within a flash, Silas trips against the current and is sitting waist-deep in the creek. He's soaked, and his laughter makes Nyla spring into imitation. Even though the sun provides much warmth at this elevation, the soaked children start to chill. With luck, I have an extra pair of clothes in the truck. After some play, we walk back to the trailhead, change clothes, and return to walking up the trail to scout the remaining areas of the location. It was fortunate that I was reminded of the cardinal rule of children and water—they almost always get wet. Learning this lesson again prompted me to include that note in my description for the upcoming event.

It's easy to be a victim when you are out in nature if you are not prepared, but to run a quality family nature club, you'll need to take some leadership in helping guests know what to expect. Scouting locations in advance is the best way to be sure that you're leading your club into territory for which they are prepared. Scouting locations does take some time, but it is one of my favorite aspects of organizing our family nature club: Things almost always go wrong (err, unexpected) when scouting, which means it's a real adventure! Having good knowledge about the location makes you a good leader, builds trust, and strengthens your community. It's a perspective that will bring you a great deal of happiness and really ensure the success of your club.

How to Scout Events for Your Family Nature Club

Your process for scouting events for your family nature club will vary a great deal based on the type of event. For outings that you are leading in nature, it is important to visit the location yourself so you are familiar with the different aspects. Even if you've been to a location before, it may have been in a different season, which could impact the options. For example, I was interested in a mountain location that I knew had ample parking, but when I went in the winter, I discovered that the last mile of the road was closed during the snowy months. For outings where a naturalist or other third party is leading, it may be less important to visit the location, but you should still meet with the person in advance.

Here are the three steps to scout an event:

Preparing consists of two aspects. The first is doing your research so you know where to go and what you might do during the event. Research was discussed in detail in the previous chapter, and the one thing to keep in mind for scouting is that you'll want to be sure you have a map, GPS, or other knowledge of how to get to where you are going. The second is bringing the right equipment. The equipment you need for scouting varies slightly from when you go out for the actual event because you don't know what to expect on your first visit. I tend to bring more clothes, food, and water in case unexpected weather conditions take us by surprise or we end up exploring longer than planned. You should also bring a camera and possibly a notepad to make a record of what you find so you can include this in your documentation.

Scouting, as I mentioned, is my one of my favorite aspects of our family nature club. Sometimes our experience goes just as planned, but often things don't turn out how we expect. I've found closed roads and dangerous waters, gone too far on trails I didn't know, come across very muddy conditions, and experienced all sorts of aspects to a location that may be unappealing for a club event. Thus, it's good to go into scouting without expectations—and, if you are bringing your family, which I like to do, to manage their expectations too. I always tell my children we're going on an "adventure" when we're scouting, and they love the freedom and surprise that brings. To scout a location, you simply go there and evaluate the location to see if it meets your goals.

Take photos of all of these aspects, ideally featuring your children in some of the shots so you can show the benefits of the location and event. I like to try to find a "hero shot" with my children at the location having a blast and showing off the most attractive aspects of the place.

Getting Permission

In some cases, you will need to contact open space, park managers, or an agency that manages the locations you want to visit due to the regulations for visitations from groups. After you've scouted a location and decide you want to visit it with your group, contact the person in charge of the location by email or phone. Introduce your group and plans, and request permission to visit their location.

Jason's Picks

What I look for when scouting:

- Parking—Is there sufficient parking for my club members?

- Challenge—How difficult will it be for my club to navigate and have the kind of experience I want? Can they do it? If not everyone can do it, how do I help them understand the difficulty?

- Hazards—Is there deep water or frozen bodies of water that might present danger? Large rocks kids might climb on? Cliffs kids could fall down? What will I need to warn parents about?

- Attractions—What kind of features will be exciting for my club? Wildlife? Scenery? Any special plants or geological formations? What will make this place fun and memorable?

- Weather—How will changing weather impact the club experience? Is there shade for hot days? Is the location susceptible to high winds? What extra clothing is required, given the time of year?

- Independence—If someone else is guiding the event, how will that work for my club members? If it is a long adult-guided activity, what will the children be drawn to that might distract the event? How can I manage this in advance? How will this vary between the age ranges of the children in our group? Can I provide options for those not interested in the event, such as breaking it up and allowing free time? Will there be nearby places for those distracted to play without getting separated from the group?

What You've Learned

In this chapter, you've learned how to scout events for your family nature club. You've learned how to prepare, visit, and evaluate locations.

CHAPTER 5

FLY

Taking a snack break on the trail to our first summit with our family nature club.

10:50 AM. We move in bursts up the trail on the western slope towards the Green Mountain summit—sometimes running, sometimes meandering. There are a dozen of us, parents and children, and every few steps one of the children discovers something to admire: a fallen pine cone, a sticky bush, the peeling bark of an evergreen, a quartz stone that stirs their imagination into fantasy play of princesses, wizards, and gnomes. The day yawns into mid-morning as other hikers pass us with ease, admiring our group even with our lollygagging pace.

Shouts and waves from the tail of our long line of nature adventurers raise our attention—new friends have found us on the trail! They arrived late, but moving with such a big group makes it easy to catch us. A celebration is in order, and we promptly sit to enjoying a buffet of dried fruit, nuts, seaweed, and water. With perfectly blue skies, moderate temperatures, and the group's pleasant energy, we make it—after hours—to the summit. Our friends who arrived late are there with us to rejoice in a reward full of vistas of the epic Rocky Mountains cascading down from the Continental Divide to the west, and to the east the plains rolling out across the horizon. Red-tailed hawks circle above us intermittently, catching drifts of warm winds, admiring the top of this great mountain. Without the right information ahead of time, our friends would not have found us and enjoyed this experience.

Your family nature club will crash and burn if you don't adequately provide the necessary information for your members. With a little bit of work, you can quickly outline details of an event and ensure high quality experiences, allowing your club to really FLY! Researching and scouting will give you the necessary information you need to document your family nature club events. Then all you have to do is write up the details!

How to Document Events for Your Family Nature Club

While the details of what you include will vary a bit, you'll find that you can use a template approach to make documenting events easy and quick. In some cases, you may be repeating an event—or doing something a very similar—which will make the process even easier. I've found that over time I got quicker and quicker at documenting (especially by using a template), so don't be too anxious if the first few times you document an event it takes longer than you hope. Writing good descriptions will make it easier for people to participate and avoid problems that you or your members will encounter being unprepared.

Informed and prepared parents are more apt to attend your events and be happy when doing so.

Giving them the right information—a day plan and checklist for a hassle-free event—in advance will increase the fun they have.

What you should include in your documentation is:

Photograph of the event that is at once descriptive and inspiring. I like to think of these as the hero shots. If you're returning to a place you have visited before, you might have a wonderful photograph you can use. If not, you can find them easily on Google or other outdoor sites.

Title of the event that includes just enough information to tell the whole story. I like to include both the type of event—such as "unstructured nature play," "hiking," or "boating," and the location. This gives your members a succinct summary that will help them determine their interests in a flash.

Date/time and expected duration of the event so that people know how the event will fit into their schedules. If you are posting your events using a system that supports start and stop time, this will be accomplished with just those two data points. Do not include driving time in the start and stop of the event because people will be arriving from different locations.

Description of the event or an **about the area** summary of the location. In both cases, I like to include why I like the activity and location, and why it is special (to help others see why they might have a good time). Spending a few minutes writing an enticing description or "about the area" section is a good way to attract people!

Hazards are always nice to include to help people properly prepare. In many cases, you might be able to omit this, but in some cases it is valuable. For example, if you're planning to explore a stream in winter time, it is helpful to remind people that children will likely get wet, and so they should bring extra shoes and clothes and waterproof boots. Or, if you are boating, you'll want to remind folks to bring life jackets, and help them figure out where to get that equipment. I like to include general notes such as calling out if there are big rocks children will likely scramble up, or if the area is notorious for high winds (in which case they should be sure to bring the right clothing to stay warm).

Where to meet, including driving directions, parking, and where the group will be while waiting for others to arrive. It is helpful to include a link to a map (such as Google Maps) that will make it easy for people to see where the parking lot is, as well as the trailhead. If the trailhead is not obvious, try to include some kind of landmark as reference, like a bridge, lake, or building. It is important in this section to let folks know about the buffer—what time to arrive and what time the event will start. For example, you should allow a 10–15 minute grace period for late arrivals; so if the plan is to meet at 9 AM, then let them know you will be departing from the meeting place at 9:10 AM or 9:15 AM.

Map of the trail or area is very helpful, especially for those who may be arriving late. Try to make a plan for where you will be going, and let people know how they might be able to find you if they arrive after the event start time. You can include specific landmarks or the names of trails you will travel; such as "we'll be taking the South Mesa Trailhead towards Shadow Canyon heading towards Bear Mountain."

Activities that you expect to take place, such as boating, hiking, or exploring. This is a good point to remind people of the type of experience you are trying to create. For example, if the event is designed as unstructured nature play, you can remind them how a child-led event works (i.e., "we'll let the children guide us, and will be moving slow"). This can help avoid frustration by parents who might be expecting a hike. For big hikes, it is helpful to include things like elevation gain, distance, whether the location is stroller friendly, etc.

What to bring in terms of clothes and food, and reminding folks to bring water. It's also nice to point out other fun things to bring, such as basic first aid kit, field books, binoculars, tools, mosquito repellant, sunscreen, sunglasses, etc.

Additional photos are always nice if you have them. These can play a big role in inspiring folks to join the event, especially if you have some photos of children having fun and doing things that they otherwise would not be able to experience.

A note on liability, and that parents are always responsible for their own children.

Contact information for the leader, including your name and mobile phone number.

NOTE: What I do not include with each event description is basics, like outdoor safety and how to be prepared for the outdoors. Prepared families are more comfortable and happy! You can provide a participant checklist when they first join your club, and for some events, such as a camping trip, you can provide additional gear checklists in addition to the event descriptions.

Jason's Picks

My event descriptions continue to evolve, but I try to follow a basic template format to make creating them more efficient. Here is an example of one of my event descriptions.

Unstructured Nature Play at Gregory Canyon Trailhead

ABOUT THE AREA

Gregory Canyon is north of the Flatirons and terminates where Baseline Road turns into Flagstaff Road near Chautauqua. The Gregory Creek corridor is known to support apple and plum trees that attract bears (I saw one here last summer) and other wildlife.

The creek is tiny but splendid, and tucked away beneath the trees and sharp incline of the canyon. The trailhead is an access point to a couple of trails heading up into the hills. When it's cold enough, the creek is frozen, and in the summer it gurgles in small pools—always wonderful and fun to explore.

HAZARDS

Because it's winter, the area and surrounding trails are slippery. They are also steep in parts, and can be challenging. Kids love it, but for those carrying babies you'll need to be mindful of where you step.

WHERE TO MEET

The Gregory Canyon Trailhead is next to the parking lot at the base of Flagstaff Mountain. There is a fee for non-Boulder County residents, unless you have a Mountain Parks pass. The parking lot is small and fills up early.

We'll meet at the trailhead from 9:00 AM to 9:10 AM. This will also be basecamp. We'll set down our stuff and the children will be able to range freely from there. However, depending on the interests of the children and group, we'll either stick around at basecamp for the whole time, exploring the creek area, or we'll hike up one of the trails—most likely some combination of the two.

Parking

At Gregory Canyon Trailhead

> www.goo.gl/maps/TcJ4Z9HyZBn
>
> www.goo.gl/maps/TcJ4Z9HyZBn

Downloadable Gregory Canyon Area Trail Map

> https://www-
> static.bouldercolorado.gov/docs/Chautauq
> ua-trail-map-1-201504171350.pdf

GETTING TO BASECAMP

If you can't park at the trailhead where basecamp is, alternative parking is at Chautauqua or along Baseline, both of which require an extra but pleasant walk across the meadow.

Alternative Parking Options

On Baseline

> www.goo.gl/maps/sqjANNtwFuC2
>
> www.goo.gl/maps/sqjANNtwFuC2

At Chautauqua

> www.goo.gl/maps/myH3jM7gJU0
>
> www.goo.gl/maps/myH3jM7gJU0

From Baseline or Chautauqua, get the Baseline Trail that runs parallel to Baseline from Chautauqua and head east towards Gregory Canyon Trailhead. It is about half a mile from Chautauqua to the trailhead, and includes a brief walk through the forest and then descending down a steep path and crossing where there used to be a bridge (washed out by the floods) to reach the creek.

This is basecamp.

If you arrive late, it may be that we have departed from basecamp, and it will be difficult to find us because we are not planning any specific route. Please RSVP so we know that you are coming.

WHAT WE'LL DO

This event is focused on unstructured nature play, but may include some hiking.

If you're new to unstructured nature play, the idea is to provide time and space for children to play, explore, and discover nature. This event has no defined goals or rules.

WHAT TO BRING

- Warm clothes and possibly a change of clothes and shoes in case of getting wet

- Water shoes for summer, winter boots or other water resistant/proof boots

- Snacks!! And WATER!

- Binoculars (optional)

- Bird, tree, animal identification books (optional)

- Animal tracking books (optional)

- Hatchet for possible ice digging (optional)

- Basic first aid supplies

Two of the children mining for ice crystals in the mountain stream. They were so pleasant in trading the hatchet back and forth.

PARENTS/CAREGIVERS ARE SOLELY RESPONSIBLE FOR THE SAFETY AND WELL-BEING OF THEIR CHILDREN AT ALL TIMES.

What You've Learned

In this chapter, you've learned how to make your family nature club events outstanding by giving participants the information they need for the specific event, and for events in general.

CHAPTER 6

POWER OF EFFICIENCY

The children huddle close in a makeshift teepee situated on woodlands dusted with snow and sunlight.

9:05 AM. Blue skies crash down upon perfectly smooth snowy surfaces—the roofs of a series of ponds that weave between woodlands and waterfowl. It's such a gorgeous day. My phone rings. It's one of the dads who is lost and needs directions to find the trailhead. I quickly reorient him. Then a text comes in. It's a mom who lets me know their family has decided to come, and wants to make sure they know how to find us. I refer her to the map I posted on our Facebook group that shows the location of the makeshift teepee, where we'll make basecamp.

9:10 AM. Several families have arrived now at the trailhead, and it's time for us to head to basecamp. We visit the ponds regularly, and the children know it well. They tear off into the woodlands; a billow of snow swooshes into the crisp morning on their heels. When we arrive to basecamp, the children spot the teepee. It's been decorated by the snow queen, they announce. They promptly burrow through slits to huddle like a tribe of elders planning an elaborate journey together in secret. Geese traipse across the horizon. It's still sub-freezing as another family and children arrive at basecamp. Their happiness is contagious as ever, and the new arrival quickly joins in the fun.

Our relationship with technology is precarious—it connects us and makes us distant. As a tool to organize and coordinate family nature club, it is invaluable. And it is efficient. Using technology allows you to reach a great number of people, keeping them informed and inspired, while optimizing your efficiency.

How and What Technology to Use to Organize Events

You need three basic tools to organize every event for your family nature club: a calendar system, a reminder system, and a contact system. I've found that you can automate these using inexpensive Web-based technologies, and that doing so really improves your success in getting people to events and having a great time there. These technologies are easy to learn and use, and you will find that, as you use them, you will get much quicker in a short amount of time. Once you've got the three systems running smoothly, you'll be very happy with how easy it is to organize your club!

The three systems you need:

Calendar System

Once you've figured out the logistics and written the descriptions for your events, the next step is to put them on a calendar. You need a calendar to make your life way easier, because it will allow you to schedule an event at a specific moment in time, and will automatically manage whether events are in the future or have already happened and are in the past. With a calendar, your club members will be able to quickly see upcoming events, and be able to put them on their own schedules. There are a lot of different options out there for calendar systems, from Google Calendar to Meetup.com to Facebook to Wordpress plugins for a blog to custom-developed calendar software that lives on your website.

Scheduling events in advance and at the same time every week/every two weeks/every month/etc. will make it easier for people to get them on their schedules. Since I like to use feedback and observation to guide future event planning, I only schedule four or five events at a time, once per week—so just over a month of events. Sometimes I have special events that must occur at a specific time, such as camping (where we need to get a reservation early). In those cases, I schedule the events some months in the future. Since writing descriptions takes time, I tend to put events on the calendar with just a photo and maybe a link to the location/venue, and add a note that "details are coming soon." This allows people to put the event on the calendar in advance. Then, as a second step, days/week(s) later I'll go in and add the details of the event.

Many calendar systems also allow the ability to duplicate past events when starting new ones. This works well if you host repeat events, saving you time in copy/pasting or rewriting things you've already crafted.

Reminder System

Many calendar systems include event reminders as part of their services. This is helpful in case someone who has registered for an event forgets or needs a gentle reminder the day before the event. The reminder systems that are part of the calendar systems vary a great deal in how exactly they work, and it's worth testing out different systems to see which one you think will work best for your members. Not all calendars have built-in reminders. For example, if you use Google Calendar to show events, club members will not be able to "register" for an event, and they will not be automatically getting a reminder even if they add it to their own calendars. If your calendar does not have reminders, you can set up an email system to send email reminders to your club members.

It's important to have reminders sent to members either the day before, or the weekday before a weekend event. If your calendar system already has this function built in, you don't have to do anything! For those using a standalone email system, such as Aweber, MailChimp, or even Gmail, it is best to write your reminder emails following a template. This will reduce your work and make it easier for users to quickly scan your emails and get the main point. The email reminders should link to the full event description or include the full description in the body of the email.

Contact System

No matter how good a calendar system and reminder system you set up, you will still have people who need assistance in getting to the event on the day of. It may be that they'll send you an email or a text asking for help. Alternately, you may have to make last-minute changes to an event. For example, if a location or activity is weather dependent, you may have to unexpectedly cancel it or make some changes to the time. In all cases, you should maintain an active contact list of your club members that includes their emails and mobile phone numbers. It is also a good idea to request emergency contact information.

You likely have your favorite way of storing contacts already, whether in your email system, on a spreadsheet, or just in a document.

Spreadsheets are efficient and allow you to import the data into various other tools. It is important to keep your contact list up-to-date, so whenever a new member joins, you should add them to this list.

How to Pick the Best Technology

What technology you ultimately decide on will vary greatly based on your own requirements. Some questions to ask yourself as you are considering the options:

1. Are you price sensitive and wanting to find something that is free, or are you OK with spending some money each month?

2. What's your level of technical comfort? Do you want to have to think about maintaining a Web application, or do you want a hosted solution?

3. How will these systems integrate with each other and any other technology you'll be using? Do you want one system, or are you OK with running a variety of technology?

4. What will your club members respond best to?

Jason's Picks

When I first started my family nature club, I started by using Meetup, because Meetup provides a nice combination of social features (picture sharing, discussions), calendar, and email communications (for event reminders). However, Meetup's settings for private groups only restrict the ability for members to automatically join your group. You can't turn off the visibility of the group, and the result was that I received more than three dozen inquiries within the first several days of being live. Since I wanted to just invite a few friends to start, I closed my Meetup group and moved to Facebook, and set up a secret group. Facebook has been OK. It has nice social features, and I can set up events pretty easily. If you're interested in setting up a public group, Meetup is great for attracting members with similar values and interests, and offers a free trial period and a low monthly cost.

Unfortunately, I've discovered that not everyone who wants to join my group is on Facebook, and they are thus not able to see the calendar. Additionally, Facebook's emailing options for groups is not fantastic. I can't be sure that my members are receiving emails about my notifications, and they often report not getting reminders (I believe they get lost in the many notifications Facebook sends). This year, I've decided to test MailChimp. This adds a bit of extra overhead administrative work for me, but I think it is much better for my club. Each week, I send one email with a reminder for the event to be held on the weekend, upcoming future events, and general announcements. It's nice to be able to email people directly, and they appreciate getting emails with the information.

In talking with other club leaders, I've heard positive feedback about Wordpress because it supports a blog and plugins can be used for the calendar, and it also has good features for privacy if needed.

What You've Learned

In this chapter, you've learned how valuable technology is for organizing and coordinating events for your family nature club. You've learned about calendar systems and email systems, and how to organize your contacts.

CHAPTER 7

DISCONNECT

*The children play on a giant log and inflatable
kayak at an idyllic summer lake.*

10:10 AM. A young girl climbs aboard the front
end of a half-submerged tree. It is amazingly
buoyant, and bounces and sways, colliding gently
with an inflatable kayak. Clasping paddles, the
children move across the shallow waters of the

lake. The kayak slides easily across the surface water, pulling away from the log and beach towards a nearby floating dock. The kayakers arrive to the shouts and celebration of children who are stranded on the dock. Children jump from the dock to the kayak and vice versa, leaving a new group of stranded children on the dock and a new crew in the kayak.

Meanwhile, onshore families enjoy sun kisses and sand toys. Infants wander up and down the beach munching on watermelon and chasing sunfishes with nets and glee. The log floats nearer and other children try their best to walk up and down the unstable float, jumping off as they lose their balance to splash into the welcoming waters. Cell phones are tucked away and adults monitor the children, periodically getting invited to partake in their goofing off and imaginary play. Be a turtle. Swim like a dolphin. Hop along as a frog. The play is infectious and everyone is connecting—with sand, water, tree bark, and each other.

Disconnecting from technology helps us focus on what's happening with those around us, and our surroundings. Being engaged during nature outings is important for every participant, and especially for leaders. As the leader, your job is to be a good host, which means putting away cell phones and interacting with the families who join your events.

How to Be a Good Host for Your Family Nature Club

Besides tucking away mobile devices, there are a variety of steps you should take as the host of your family nature clubs. These will vary depending on whether your group is made up entirely of regulars who are familiar with how events are run, or if you're welcoming first-timers to your event. It will also vary whether you are guiding the event solely or if there is a third party involved, such as a naturalist, skills leader, or other educator. There are four basic steps you should take for every event.

The four ways to be a good host:

Welcome and Introduction

When families arrive to your events, you need to welcome them. As mentioned, you should allow for a 10- to 15-minute grace period for latecomers. By welcoming folks as they arrive, it helps people know they are in the right place, and also makes them feel like they're showing up to something they are part of. As each family first arrives, it is a good idea to greet people. Introduce yourself and make introductions to other guests. Some groups and/or events require nametags. If you plan on doing that, it's best to get guests to put nametags on right away. Depending on your group structure, you may also want to record the number of participants at each event, collect contact information, and get them to fill out the liability release forms.

It is very important that, as the host, you arrive on time, and that you start the event on time after the grace period. This will help build confidence in your guests and ensure repeat attendance.

Once everyone has arrived and the grace period is over, to officially start the event you should gather everyone around for a quick introduction. You can keep this as casual as pointing out where you're heading and announcing that it's time to start, or you can have a more in-depth introduction. Here are some of what can be included in a more in-depth introduction:

- Group norms/principles—Remind the guests of your group's norms and principles. You can talk about the purpose of your group, such as connecting with nature, giving the children free time and space for unstructured play, or encouraging skill building. You can keep a printout of your group's norms and principles and read it to them as a gentle reminder.

- Intention/direction—Inform guests as to the plan for the day. Talk about what you expect to happen, and where there is flexibility in that plan. For example, you might be going on a hike and have a specific goal in mind, or maybe you are leading an "unhike" where the point is not to get anywhere, but instead to follow the children's whims rather than adult urges. If you're doing something like boating, let them know what kind of equipment is available, and how to use it.

- Risks/rules—Talk about what kind of risks there are at the event location, or associated with the specific activity. If there are poisonous plants, dangerous animals, or environmental conditions (high rocks, ice, strong currents, etc.), let them know how to avoid any problems, and what to do if a problem arises. Some events will have specific rules that you should make guests aware of. For example, you may be visiting a farm that uses electric fencing that is not particularly pleasant to touch. Or, you may be in a nature or wildlife preserve with sensitive environment where off-trail exploration is not allowed.

- Caregiving—Discuss how each parent is responsible for their own children. Talk about what happens if some children want to split up. It may be that parents are comfortable with watching other children, but remind folks that it is up to the parents to ensure they get permission or agreement from others before assuming someone is watching their children.

- Staying engaged—This is a good time to remind people to put away their technology and stay engaged with their children, their family, and others.

Deepening Relationships

Help strengthen your community by taking an active role in deepening relationships. Take an interest in the other families, and work to get to know them by talking to each adult and child throughout the event. When speaking with children, it is a good idea to crouch down so that your eyes are at the same level as theirs. You can make much-appreciated introductions between families that don't know each other well by giving some background on you and how you know the other people. You can spark conversations with small talk starters by asking people about their own childhoods, experiences in nature, or interests in attending the event or joining the group.

Guiding

As the leader of your family nature club, you are the logistical coordinator for your group. Besides mapping out the plan for the day, while you're at your event, you are the one people will look to for direction as to what to do. From guiding activities like icebreakers to bringing special equipment such as guidebooks, magnifying glasses, and binoculars, to literally guiding the group in a location, you should assume a leadership role in helping move the event along. In the cases when a third party is leading the event, you should still welcome and introduce the event, as well as work towards deepening relationships. But you can depend more heavily on this third party to do the guiding for the day. There may also be natural leaders in your group who will make suggestions as to the direction or activity to pursue. You can welcome these suggestions and follow them, or remind them of a different plan that you want to pursue. Guiding is a delicate balance of telling people what to do—for example, informing everyone that you're going to explore up a creek—modeling, and showing them that you're stopping by putting your stuff down and starting to play. It's also important to get feedback from others to gauge everyone's interest and comfort level. If you re on a rigorous hike and trying to stay together, you can survey people at various points to see if folks are ready to turn around or keep going. Don't worry if you have no experience guiding—just try out different approaches and see what works best for you and the group. What's most important is your enthusiasm and empathy for others!

Staying Safe

Paramount to the success of your family nature club is staying safe. This starts with how you pick and organize events, including scouting locations to ensure you understand the risk associated with each event. While the responsibility of a child's safety belongs to their parents, it is important to help parents stay aware of current dangers and risks, and help point out when problems are arising. If you're on a trail with large rocks, it's a good idea not to let children climb so high that a fall could be life changing in a bad way. Likewise, playing near water introduces many risks that you should be aware of, so take appropriate considerations. You can research risky play and how to manage that in advance of your group to get more information. In a later chapter, I will discuss legal protection to keep you and your families safe.

Jason's Picks

My style for hosting our family nature club events is shaped by having a small private group of families who all currently attend or have attended the same school. We know each other well, and so the group's norms and event styles are all very well known. I run my events more casually than I would if it was a public group where new members were joining each week. So my welcome and introduction is more like what you would expect at an afternoon picnic. Some people arrive on time, while others join a little later. We aren't so formal as starting each event with an official welcome introduction, but rather I spend a lot of time while on the trail talking with other parents about options for how to let the event unfold.

I have a light-handed approach to guiding, and focus a great deal of effort on making sure that guests have as good a time as possible—including both children and parents. I try to interact with everyone during the event.

I stay alert and keep other parents alert to any safety issues, both before and during the event. While I support and help facilitate risky play, I work to ensure that any risky play is low consequence. So, for example, we may play on a half-frozen creek with a high chance of the children breaking through and getting wet, but it is on warmer days, with extra clothes, and with parents staying close to children and not wandering far from our vehicles (rather than playing on a deep lake with thin ice where falling through is very dangerous and high consequence).

What You've Learned

In this chapter, you've learned how disconnecting with technology will allow you to be a better host and focus on what is important—the people and experience! You've learned about how to welcome and introduce events, how to deepen relationships, how to guide, and how to stay safe for your family nature clubs.

CHAPTER 8

STAY SAFE

Nyla on hands and knees, trying to recover from hitting her head on the ice.

10:48 AM. All winter she had wanted to go ice skating, but when we finally made it up to the lake her legs were unsteady, like anyone trying something again for the first time in years. Other children and families slid across the ice with ease just as Nyla's feet flew out from under her, and she fell down against the ice. With a sickening thud, her head hit and ricocheted off the surface of the frozen lake. The pain was so intense that she struggled for a breath and climbed to her knees. After a beat, the tears flowed, then the whimpers. She then pronounced that she never wanted to skate again. I quietly thought to myself . . . *we have to do this more often*. The moment passed and the families with us made for a delightful day skating at the mountain lake.

The learning curve for ice skating is steep. Often, young ones will use some kind of stabilizer on the ice when they are first starting out, but the beautiful clear blue skies and warming days at the lake saw high numbers of people, and few stabilizers were available. Nearby, hockey players wore helmets, and I wondered if I'd made a mistake not having Nyla wear one.

How to Protect Yourself As the Leader

Being in nature and the outdoors does carry some risk. The previous chapters have discussed a variety of ways to help mitigate injuries that children—or adults—may incur while participating in your family nature club, but there is still the chance that something more serious may happen. You should take some steps to protect yourself and your members. In addition, it is always a good idea to get permission from participants to use photos you take of them, whether on your blog, website, social media accounts, or other marketing materials.

Here are three things you should do:

Have all members sign a photo and liability release before they participate in any event. You can facilitate this online or offline (at the event), or through a combination of both. Many family nature clubs have operated for years and years using just this precaution. If you're running a public group, you can make registering for the group and signing a waiver the first step someone must take before they are allowed to view the calendar and register for events. Using an online survey tool such as Survey Monkey will make this very efficient. For folks who happen to show up without having filled out the release, you can carry a clipboard with extra copies of releases to have them sign up before participating.

Don't feel awkward asking for this! Your release can be written with the intention of not just protecting you as the leader, but also protecting other parents from being liable to other participants. Many organized indoor and outdoor events, summer camps and programs, field trips, and other school programs all require participants to sign releases.

Include a note about responsibility on all event descriptions, as you have seen in the example in the previous chapter. This can just be a simple sentence that reminds parents and caregivers of who has responsibility for their child. This is a great extra precaution on top of the release.

Consider liability insurance. Depending on the structure of your organization, you may want to consider getting liability insurance. Liability insurance is not inexpensive, and may require that you charge your members a monthly fee to participate. If your family nature club is part of a larger existing organization, they may already have liability insurance. If you end up wanting to create a legal entity such as a non-profit or LLC for your family nature club, this may be more important to look into.

In some cases, specific locations or activities may require group liability insurance.

Jason's Picks

When I first started my club, I envisioned it as simply a small group of friends getting together, and I didn't do anything in the way of liability. As it has grown, in just the past few months, I have started to use a photo and liability release, as well as including a note of responsibility on all my group descriptions.

To make filling out the release form quick and easy for my members, I use the online survey tool Survey Monkey. The survey is short and consists of just a few questions that can be answered quickly by a parent or caretaker. I send the link to new members before I add them to our Facebook group. Members have been very amicable, and some members have even complimented the addition of the release because they feel it gives them some protection as well.

Since my club is small and I add new members infrequently, I don't have a need to bring release forms to the actual events, and have yet to look into liability insurance.

What You've Learned

In this chapter, you've learned how to use photo and liability releases, and when to consider liability insurance for your family nature club.

CHAPTER 9

ATTACHMENT AND DESIRE

The children navigate a mountain stream, crossing en route to warmer lands.

9:23 AM. Silas stands, staring at the group of older children who have climbed 20 or 30 feet up the sharply angled snow-drenched mountain. He is only three years old, and still loses his footing every now and then, so I wonder if allowing him to continue this journey is appropriate. The other older children scrambled up easily and perch on fallen logs, boulders, and the steep slope. As Silas climbs higher and higher, I fight back the growing urges to rush up there and spot him. He's a Scorpio, so approaching him would likely draw screams of "I can do it!" Yet my mind conjures up visions of him tumbling and hitting his head on granite rocks, or rolling into a broken evergreen bough. Thinking about all the research I've seen on how risky play is healthy, I somehow resist my desire to help. Some minutes later, he makes it all the way up. But how will he get down? What have I done? A beat later, he turns, sits on his bum, and slides down the snowy hill, making a parade of joy as he goes. He's very, very happy. My heart swells.

Minutes later, the pack of children have made their way to the edge of a pool of water with a collection of fallen logs that make a crossing over the mountain stream. We are deep in this frozen canyon, pushing towards a faraway goal. One after another, the children navigate the logs, delicately balancing as they make their way to the south-facing slope that presents the spots of sunshine. We're hoping to reach the warmer patches soon to warm our bodies up, but fording the creek introduces risk of the children dipping their feet and legs into the alpine waters. Our events consistently present opportunities for children to test their limits, and the limits of their parents trailing close behind. We've grown comfortable with allowing risk-taking, and it has produced amazing personal growth for the children.

Being attached to outcomes and the desire to protect your kids is at odds with giving them opportunities to be independent and build character, confidence, and strength. It requires letting go of control and focusing on allowing your events to be child-led as much as possible. With a few basic rules of thumb, this can be easily achieved.

How to Lead Child-Led Events

Inherently, child-led events are not adult-guided, so your role as a leader and parent is to ensure the children have the space and support they need to successfully "guide" themselves. In many ways, this is the basics of being a Hummingbird Parent. While not every family nature club event will be wholly child-led—like an educational or skill-building event, hiking, or other more goal-oriented outings—you can still maintain a sense of being child-led with a few simple steps.

Here are the six steps:

Maintain a safe environment by understanding the risks associated with the activity and location. This includes having the right clothing, equipment, and skills, and keeping a watchful eye on what's happening so you can anticipate problems before they happen. Once at a certain age, children are adept at managing their own risks of what they understand. Cuts, bruises, and broken bones may be acceptable risk, but being sure to help children navigate risk that carries greater consequence is vital. For example, children are capable of climbing rocks much higher than would be safe to fall from. Likewise, they may be eager to walk across ice that could result in very dangerous situations if it cracked. Learning to use knives and fires, boating, and exploring the ocean are examples of where you need to be involved to ensure a safe environment and experience.

Providing prompts for exploratory, imaginative, and creative experience is easy and fun for adults. Simply find things that you think the children will find novel, interesting, or engaging, and call their attention to them. You can introduce things in a variety of ways, such as naming a bird, plant, or rock, telling a brief story of the animal that may have left a track, or talking about tree rings and other landscape or geological features. I frequently bring binoculars, field guides, and tools like hatchets and pocketknives as invitations for the children. Focusing on small details is a great way to spur children's imaginations.

Allow children to follow their own agendas, and don't force your own agenda on them. This is probably the biggest challenge in our very goal-oriented culture. It is useful to explain this idea to the parents and other adults in your group before (such as in your event descriptions) and at the start of the outing. Even when the event includes an educational or skill-building aspect, it's important to combine it with some free play or unstructured play, which gives children the chance to be independent. The practice of allowing children to follow their own agendas is not unlike meditation—you need to be quiet and avoid interrupting their play.

Observing from a distance is a balancing act, taking into consideration your role of maintaining a safe environment. At times, you'll need to be within arm's reach of children, like if you're crossing a raging river or climbing high. But generally, you should back away from the gaggle of children to give them the space they need to move about physically on their own. This gives them the freedom to explore, follow their agendas, and have their own experiences with the other children.

Acting (upon request) as a character in children's role-playing can be really fun! Be prepared and willing to get down on your hands and knees in the dirt, mud, and water! Be silly! Channel your inner child. This is your chance to be an honorary child, and if you do it right, you will be greatly rewarded. But stay in character! To be successful, bear in mind that your role is to support and facilitate their experience. Allow children to be the leaders, and you their humble servant. This is a bit of a role reversal from the typical adult-child relationship, and really enhances their play. Simply wait for an invitation.

Introduce new ideas through questions or briefly modeling behavior by observing the activities of the tribe of children. Each child plays differently, and some environments and activities will work better for some children than others. In some cases, a muddy pool will provide an opportunity for one child to master a new skill, whereas other children may quickly grow bored. It's helpful to be aware of the overall engagement of the group. If it starts to wane, that's the point at which you can model behavior to redirect the energy of the children. I often will model behavior to direct children up a stream or trail, or to a new location by simply moving them myself with an announcement that I just found something cool to look at. Likewise, if you start examining something and asking questions about it, you will find children magnetized by your interest.

Jason's Picks

Before every outing, I think about what kind of experiences the children may find engaging, and then I think about what will help support their interests. During the outing, I constantly keep an eye out for safety, and interact with the children in an ebb and flow sort of way, with a focus on a few general questions:

- Where and what should we explore?

- What animal and plant life are around that would be fun to think about?

- What skills could we be trying or learning?

- What is novel here that we should examine?

- Who could be having more fun, and what can I do to help them engage?

- What imaginary play is possible here?

- Would the group enjoy moving or staying put?

What You've Learned

In this chapter, you've learned how to lead child-led events for your family nature club.

CHAPTER 10

LOVE

Nyla stands on a washed-out bridge, peering over a mountain stream as we await other families' arrival.

9:25 AM. My daughter and son kick at water and mull about, staring at small pebbles that spin and twirl down a mountain stream. The skies are grey—unusual for sunny Boulder, Colorado. We have all our standard gear: extra shoes and clothes, a barrage of snacks, a pair of binoculars, and pocketknives. The place we're at was once a parking lot nestled deep in a canyon, but since the floods last summer the road and trailhead have been greatly transformed. Today it is wild, teeming with nooks to explore and un-manicured trails. But something isn't right. The children were anticipating friends to show up, and they are disappointed. I'm disappointed, too. It takes a good amount of work to set up these events, and it's a bummer when no one shows up.

I decide to start to play and see if I can lift their spirits. First I pick up small pebbles and throw them into a pool. They make a tiny sipping sound. I scour the small beach between fingers of the stream for larger rocks. I pick up and toss a few. They make a big gulping sound as they careen into the waters. It distracts my children from their disappointment, and slowly they join me. I announce that I'm fishing—yes, fishing—with rocks. I'm trying to catch a mountain fish, the kind that likes to eat really big rocks. The bigger the rocks, the bigger the mountain fish I'll catch, I say. My children's spirits rise a bit. We've discovered a little game and some imaginary play, and it holds their attention. Shortly, one dad and his daughters show up. My children are thrilled for the company. They introduce the stone throwing game to the newcomers, and soon we're exploring up the creek, moving from one pool to another, up the fingers of the stream, along the muddy banks, balancing on teetering rocks and logs, discovering the magic of this wild place.

Crafting something from scratch takes commitment and perseverance. It takes your love. Getting your events on other families' calendars doesn't happen instantly, especially when the events require extra work for the parents that they could easily avoid by staying at home, going to a manufactured play experience, or putting their kids into an organized drop-off program. Family nature clubs inherently demand more from the parents, since they are responsible for their children and can't just drop them off with a third-party caretaker. By staying heart-centered and focusing on what you're trying to accomplish—making a lifestyle for your children— you can easily get through events with lackluster attendance. But it is worth having a plan.

How to Handle Low-Attendance Events

It's almost a guarantee that you'll have events where no one or very few people will make it out. Your role as the leader is to ensure that you still have an amazing time. You're doing this is for the children, and what the children need is the time and space and interaction with nature. Whether it's just with your child or children, or only a few others, there are three things that you can focus on in these situations:

Stay positive, even if your group's attitude starts to get negative. Remember, your intentions were to plan and attend the event—and you've accomplished that! As the leader, it's good to remind your group of these intentions too, making sure that they understand that families are busy, that unexpected things happen with parents and children, and that just because others didn't show up doesn't mean they didn't want to or won't in the future. You are exactly where you are supposed to be, and the people who show up are the right people to have shown up. Maintaining a lack of attachment to attendance is good for your emotional well-being as a leader—don't let it slow you down!

Play, explore, and get engaged! Sometimes when less people show up the group can spiral into non-action, especially if some of the more active and extroverted families haven't showed up. You should more immediately start modeling behavior to kick-start the children's own play. If this isn't something you are naturally inclined towards, one easy way to begin is to simply crouch or sit down where you are and find something of interest that is within your reach. Focus on the small—leaves, twigs, rocks, bugs—and start to touch, see, and smell what is in front of you. Start some imaginary play, pick a character, and announce what you are and what you are doing. This is what I was doing by throwing rocks into the stream, pretending I was fishing.

Create marketing materials for future events at this location. It may be that this time few people showed up, but perhaps if they saw how much fun the children have at this place, they would be more likely to come next time. Take notice of your surroundings and the activities the children participate in. Take mental or physical notes and take pictures. Photographs are by far one of the most effective marketing tools for your family nature club, and while you may have taken some when you were scouting, it's hard to capture the real experience of children during your scouting trips. Photographs are also a great way to jog your memory later of an amazing experience. If there are less people at this event, just imagine what drew you to this place that might draw others, and try to document it. You can share these as part of your future event descriptions and it will inspire more to come in the future.

Jason's Picks

Because my family nature club is private and I only invite families that attend my children's school, I've had several events that had pretty low attendance. When I had an event with just one other family, it was pretty disheartening. But I remembered my intentions and focused on loving what we were doing and what we were about. I worked hard to keep my small group's spirits high, doing all three of the things mentioned above. We ended up having an amazing time, and afterward were very glad that we had not given up before others arrived. Now that we've been doing our club for almost a year, I am more confident that people will show up. But there are always a few minutes when I first arrive and others haven't, and I wonder if anyone will actually come. My children also have this experience, and so I am always focused on these three activities to ensure that, even if no one shows up, we still have a remarkable time out in nature.

What You've Learned

In this chapter, you've learned what to do for low-attendance family nature club events.

CHAPTER 11

SMALL WINS

Nyla emerges from the creek waters as she swims under a fallen tree.

11:34 AM. It's a balmy summer day in Boulder, CO, and the children are exploring and playing in the creek. Along most stretches of this section of the creek the water is shallow, sliding across tumbled stones and along a gentle bank. This allows the children to make their way upstream and down, like explorers discovering new lands. They come upon small pools and eddies where water spiders skip across the surface of the water. Every now and then, gaggles of ducks are startled and take to the air, flapping their wings to lift off the creek and into the warm air. Leafs and twigs make excellent boat-building materials. Longer sticks are foraged and become walking poles to steady the children as they wade, splash, and march into the wilds.

Around a bend, the bank grows steeper, the creek narrower, and the water deeper. A newly fallen tree catches the children's attention. By now, Nyla and Silas have shed much of their clothes, save for their bathing suits and water shoes that allow them to enter and move in the rocky creek bed with ease. Nyla moves closer to the log and submerges to shoulder depth. Then, with amazingly great zest, she plunges into the current. Just as she's about to come to the log, she ducks underwater. She zips beneath the log and then her head lifts to see that she's made it! Only two other families are here today, but it's enough to make for an incredibly engaging and inspiring nature experience. The children spend hours mucking about, and I take the time to document the adventure.

As discussed in the last chapter, building anything from scratch can make your ego take a beating. You can expect that you'll have disappointments along the way, but if you become well practiced at emphasizing and celebrating the small wins, you'll find that you are able to achieve big results—strengthening the interest in your club by your children, your family, and your potential members. In a lot of ways, this comes down to marketing.

How to Market Your Family Nature Club

In the last chapter, you learned about the value of taking notes and photographs of your event as a way to produce marketing materials. These marketing materials are an excellent way to share the experiences you've had in past events to inspire families to join future events. You can see examples of how stories and images are used in all kinds of marketing materials, from travel companies to educational organizations and programs to summer camps and recreation companies, and even family nature clubs. By spending a little time preparing your materials and then posting and sharing these materials, stories, and tips, you will be able to raise engagement and attendance, and strengthen the bonds of your community.

The five steps to market your club include:

Researching how others are marketing their efforts will give you a great sense of what works and what doesn't work. For example, you'll see a wide range of photography, from group shots to candid action shots to focusing on documenting specific educational activities and artifacts from nature like the flora and fauna of the region. Similarly, how people share general tips, upcoming events, and stories of their adventures—the style and aesthetic—will vary greatly from simple captions to short-form stories to longer blog posts and articles. You will also see a range of tone, from commercial-looking productions to casual sharing. Find what resonates with you from other groups that you appreciate, and that will inspire your efforts.

Design your content with care. It takes practice, persistence, and commitment. While taking notes and shooting photographs was discussed in the last chapter, the additional step that is required is the post-production of these materials. Specifically, you should write up stories and process your photographs. How you write the stories will depend greatly on what inspired you in your research, and the strategy you select for posting and sharing your content. It may be that you want to share just photos. Or, maybe you want to write short stories for specific photographs and share those one at a time over a period of time. Or, perhaps you're interested in writing blog posts or articles that incorporate all the details from your experience. You can also do a combination of these. What's important is to take some time to think about what you can manage, and then to stay consistent with your approach so that your members know what to expect and grow to appreciate it. If you create print materials, you'll need to prepare those now as well. This sounds like a lot of work, but you will find it is really enjoyable, and you can start simply with small efforts. Small efforts build up and begin to snowball over time!

Publish your content in a way that attendees of the event, those who missed it, and potential future guests will be able to view. The approach here will vary based on how you communicate with your group, and can include your website, social media channels, or newsletters. In some cases, you may want to post your content immediately after you've created it. If you manage your group by Facebook or Meetup, perhaps you will want to share some images of the day's event as soon as possible. Alternately, you can plan to share your content over a period of time, such as the week following the event. This can be made easier if you use a content publishing tool to automate the process of scheduling and posting the content.

For print materials, you will need to print them out either on your home printer or at a print shop.

Share your content once it has been published. In some cases, you may not need to do anything here. If you run a blog or social media platform, those tools often will automatically send a notice to your members or subscribers letting them know that something new has been published. In other cases, you may need to send some kind of notification to your members by email or some other method. If you send out weekly event reminders and newsletters, you can include links to your published content to increase how many people are aware of your content.

For print materials, you'll need to distribute them. For example, you can place stacks of standard 8.5" x 11" fliers or colorful postcard-like fliers in local libraries, nature centers, schools, recreation centers, etc. People are used to finding community programs through these types of materials, and you will find that many people will discover your club that way.

Interact with members who find your content interesting. For example, many of the platforms you can choose from including commenting and liking features. While these may seem silly, they foster community and encourage people to stay engaged and connected even when they are not at an event. To make your job easier here, you can batch your interactions by setting a specific time each day to review what members have said something about your content.

Jason's Picks

I've been amazed at the value designing, publishing, and sharing content brings to our family nature club. My small group interacts a great deal with the content, and reflecting and remembering the shared experience brings joy to me, my children, my family, and my community. I've started to see that other members are starting to participate in taking photos, sharing stories, and contributing to the marketing materials—all without any encouragement from me. I've also been really excited to see how the content touches those who did not attend the event. I've had families who couldn't make the specific date/time of an event be inspired by our photographs and stories, and independently visited the location to have the same experience. I've also had people voice complaints when I didn't share photo memories of the event—they love seeing the photos!

My practice for creating marketing materials has evolved over time, and today consists of the following approach:

- I make sure that anyone who comes to an event has filled out the photo release, and if they do not agree to allow me to photograph them, I respect that.

- Prior to events, I review marketing materials of other organizations that seem successful. I look at their websites, brochures, and social media channels to see what content gets the highest interaction and most resonates with me.

- During events, I spend some time taking notes and photographs of our experience. I try not to be like the paparazzi (shooting photos non-stop), because I also want to be engaged during the events, and participate. This means I do miss some amazing moments, but it's an important balance to maintain, I believe.

- After events, I will post all of the photos from the event in a photo album on Facebook and share in our general discussion thread. Posting in the general discussion thread makes it easy to see the photos without going into a specific event, both instantly and in the future. I also tag anyone who was at the event, as well as their significant other if they did not attend to ensure they get a notice from Facebook. When I post here on Facebook, I am sure to include a brief note about how I felt about the event. What did we do? What were the favorite activities for the children? I am also very careful to include a note of gratitude thanking everyone for coming. They don't have to spend their free time with me and my family and the club, and I am very thankful for their presence, as it enriches my children's experience.

- Throughout the week following the event, I schedule short stories and images to post on Instagram. I use the free version of Hootsuite to manage scheduling, and post to both Instagram and my personal Facebook. Using Hootsuite allows me to batch process the work, which I usually do on Monday night, the day after our event.

- Each week, I send out an email newsletter to my group using MailChimp announcing the upcoming event on the weekend. In addition, I send out infrequent general announcement emails to my whole group. In these emails, I include links to where I posted the photos from the experience.

I don't do much in the way of print materials because I'm leading a small group that is easily reached electronically.

Note: I always try to balance out my digital work on my family nature club to be at night after the children have already gone to sleep. This allows me to spend my free time playing and interacting with my children, and being outside as much as possible, versus taking time during the day to work on these tasks.

What You've Learned

In this chapter, you've learned how to emphasize small wins for big results for your family nature club events.

CHAPTER 12

LISTEN TO TRUTH

Nyla and I give thumbs up on a new location we're scouting while Silas (on the right) rides out a wave of stubbornness-I-won't-walk-in-waist-high-snow-drifts.

10:30 AM. Nyla and Silas have wandered from the trailhead through deep snow to the gurgling sound of a mountain creek. The creek can't be seen, but we can hear it running under towers of snowdrifts and rock outcroppings. The creek runs between two mountainsides, pivoting around large evergreen trees and a trail that crisscrosses the frozen waters. Up ahead, a bridge invites us deep into the forest. With more than a foot of snow blanketing the trail, this alpine landscape appears like a winter wonderland, and seems like the perfect place to explore with our club. But suddenly Silas has stopped moving.

It's hard to know when to step back and give children space so they can grow, and when to swoop in for the rescue. The emotional exterior of my son, Silas, swells up and down like the ocean. He sheds a tear after asking to be picked up and his wishes were not granted. Moments later, he stubbornly stands and continues walking in the snowy mountains for another hour. Later, when I reminded him of how sullen he was, he smiles like a rascal, and smugly reminded *me* that he had wanted to be carried. While our scouting expedition was not entirely smooth, we're excited to have discovered a new place for our family nature club, and we owe it all to one of our members who suggested the spot.

Listening to your members is one of the best ways to generate vitality for your family nature club. Besides listening during events to ensure people are having a good time, you can solicit feedback from your members on ideas for future activities and locations. If you listen and then act upon this feedback, you will create events that families will want to participate in, and generate the vitality needed to keep your group going.

How to Solicit and Use Feedback to Shape Your Family Nature Club

The process for getting and using feedback from your members will vary depending on your personality and the personalities of your members. It will also vary depending on the purpose of your club, in that not all feedback you get will be aligned with the goals of your activities. There are different types of questions that you can ask, different ways to ask for feedback, and a variety of approaches for acting upon this feedback. Each one is discussed here briefly.

Here are two types of questions you can use to gather feedback:

A close-ended question is a format that limits responses to a fixed list of answers, such as a yes or no question or multiple-choice question. This is an effective question format when you are trying to decide between known alternatives. For example, if you want to gauge interest in specific types of events, you can ask members to give input on what events they want to see organized from a given list of options. The responses to close-ended questions can help you better understand the interests of the majority members, and prioritize events. I find it especially helpful if I want to plan an event that requires fees or equipment and I'm not sure if my group is interested in paid events or has the necessary gear to participate in an event.

An open-ended question is a format that cannot be answered with a simple "yes" or "no," or with a specific piece of information. This is an effective question format to discover new ideas or unknown preferences of a group. For example, if you are not sure what kind of events or locations to plan, you can ask people to share ideas for events. You can also gather suggestions for how to make future events more hassle-free. The responses to open-ended questions can help you in the brainstorming process to shape future events, and also as a starting point for close-ended questions.

How to ask the questions:

There are many ways to pose questions to your group, and often a combination of several approaches is most effective to get the widest range of possible respondents. Here are some of the ones that work well:

- Ask members in person. This can be a casual conversation, such as bringing up an open-ended question during an event, or it can be more formal, such as passing around a clipboard with a short comment and suggestion form at the end of an event.

- Ask members via an announcement. You can include questions as part of an email newsletter, or on a webpage. Some group management tools like Facebook and Meetup have poll features that you can use for close-ended questions. You can also post a discussion thread in most websites, and ask people to write responses to close-ended or open-ended questions by commenting on the thread.

- Ask members via direct digital communication. You can send an email, chat, or post a direct message in a forum. This can be made more efficient if you're using some kind of email service that sends out the question in bulk to users.

- Ask members via an online survey. There is a wide variety of free survey tools you can use to get feedback on open-ended or close-ended questions. You simply create the survey and then send a link to people directly, or by posting it on your community webpage. This can be an effective way to survey larger groups of people with minimal effort.

How to use feedback:

Getting feedback alone is not all that helpful. But you can act upon this feedback to make your next event more fun and hassle-free, making feedback very profound.

Here's how to use the feedback that you get:

When you discover the majority interest in something, this allows you to effectively plan future events and know that they will appeal to the majority of your club members. This is a big confidence booster, because people will self-select their participation, and you know that the event will draw interest because people have told you so.

When you discover a minority interest in something, this allows you to prioritize events properly. Depending on your lineup of events, you may decide that too few people are interested in an event, and you'll put it on the back burner. Or you can use this information to plan the low-interest-type events at a less frequent rate than other events.

When ideas are aligned with your group's purpose, you now have a great list of things you can plan for upcoming events! You can still test ideas with your group by doing a multiple-choice survey or poll to understand how much of the group is interested in this new idea.

When ideas are not aligned with your group's purpose, you now have a better understanding of the different interests of your members. You can use this information to decide what direction to grow your club, or you can use it as an opportunity to remind those specific members of the purpose of your club, and why you do or do not want to plan a certain type of event or activity.

The value of soliciting and using feedback from members cannot be overstated. This is a great way to ensure that you plan events that members enjoy, and makes your job easier in coming up with great ideas. If your club is associated with a larger organization or one that has a specific venue for activities, you may have less opportunity to shape events from this feedback—

in which case, it is a great opportunity to remind those members of the purpose of your club. As well, you can also point members to other nearby clubs or associations that might better meet those specific needs.

Jason's Picks

I've been very fortunate to have a group of folks who share my interests and also have different knowledge of good activities and locations for our events. I tend to talk to my group a lot during our events, asking both close-ended and open-ended questions to participants out in the field. This has led to great brainstorming sessions during snack time, and has given me many great ideas for upcoming events. Sometimes I will share specific problems I'm trying to work out. One time, some of my group expressed an interest in visiting an indoor climbing gym. While this is a bit outside of my group's purpose of getting into nature, it presents a good way to build skills that the children can later take into nature, sort of like learning to swim at an indoor swimming pool. I asked members if they knew of any good climbing gyms, and learned of a fantastic one that we now visit frequently. The other thing I do is post polls on my Facebook group pages to get a sense of what people are most interested in. In these polls,

I'll present just three or four event options, and ask people to rank which ones they are most interested in doing. Since some of the event options require gear (such as backpacking and boating), it is very effective to see who is interested in going. I also use my newsletters to post general thoughts about upcoming event types (such as introducing naturalist or primitive skill-building events), and ask for feedback in the email. I've found that I'll get responses to these emails, and also that the topic will come up in conversation at a later event. Besides talking in person with folks, I will chat with them via instant message at times, about ideas for upcoming events. I even had one father ping me late at night saying he'd love to have more hiking events to get his kids some exercise. I used this as an opportunity to convey to the member that getting exercise wasn't a sole focus of the event, and that at the current age of our children I thought unstructured nature play was a better value for them, and included some exercise. Since I hike a lot and know the local area, I shared a few ideas for hiking that that member could do outside of our group events. It also prompted me to plan a hike as an upcoming event.

What You've Learned

In this chapter, you've learned how to listen to what your group is saying and use that information to increase the vitality of your family nature club.

CHAPTER 13

AUDACIOUS DREAMS

Carrying my boy up the trail.

11:00 AM. Valentine's Day, 2016. A couple dozen figures meander along the foothills, planting their feet one in front of the other. We're not following any set of instructions. There aren't written rules. The sun wakes slowly, dripping rays that caress our faces.

On this holiday, we often think of those we cherish, and as we walk up the trail I look around and see families coming together to create and enjoy a community. After hiking for a couple of hours in the foothills and forest, we return to the trailhead and the children play freely in the shallow creek. Just last year, I didn't know any of these parents or their children. My dream of creating a loving, consistent, sustainable group of people interested in getting their children outside for nature-based experiences has come true. It's a magical feeling. The responsibility of leading this group still feels overwhelming at times, even now, even as I witness the dream in reality and am more confident that I can do it.

Audacious dreams have a lot of power. They can be crushing, or they can supercharge your life. Like the law of attraction, really big dreams tend to have magnetic power and a snowballing effect; you just have to achieve liftoff. One thing successful people have in common is that they understand that tackling immense challenges—achieving liftoff—is accomplished the same way you accomplish anything: one small step at a time. Perhaps you have a dream of starting your own family nature club. Perhaps you're dreaming about all the benefits it will bring to your children, your family, and you, but are just too overwhelmed to start. If so, this is the chapter for you. Once you master this small technique, you will be amazed at how your audacious dreams enrich your life.

How to Build Your Family Nature Club One Skill at a Time

Your process to build your family nature club will vary a great deal based on your background, experience, time, and network. You may already have experience organizing groups, and so will find that part of organizing family nature clubs easy. Or maybe you don't, but are very technically savvy, so setting up websites and email marketing is the easy part for you. Or maybe none of that is going to be easy, but you are setting up your family nature club for an existing organization, so attracting members will be easy. In my experience, most people are really good at some things and not good at other things. It's important to recognize this and understand that you don't need to be perfect at everything when you start. You can build your skills along the way. Here's how:

Start at the right size to ensure that you can handle the group organization effectively. By size, I mean not just the number of participants, but also the frequency and diversity of events. These three things will greatly determine the amount of time and effort required to effectively plan, organize, and create great events. Keep in mind that before you were a parent you might have been able to handle more. So, for example, let's say you have never organized a group before, and have two young kids. Maybe this means you should start with just a few friends and test out your capabilities with planning one event a month. If you have a lot of experience organizing events and you are doing this for a large existing organization with much of the infrastructure already in place, maybe you want to start with two events each week and as many people as want to sign up. It really depends, but it's better to start small and create something of quality that you can handle. You can always grow it once you have the quality in place.

Launch the beta version that isn't perfect. The first step is the hardest. No matter what, if this is your first time doing a family nature club, the events are not going to be perfect. Accept that, and start with the rough draft, the beta version, the event that you'll look back on later in life and say, "Well, that was a little bumpy, but it worked!" What parts of your club can you skip to just start this week or weekend? What is the minimum that you need? Can you skip everything discussed in this book except finding a location and inviting a few friends? That should work at least for a few events, and then you can start building it. Don't be afraid of starting too small—just start!

Master skills, and then automate so that you can expand your family nature club. Of course you can't automate everything, but if you start by just emailing friends, you'll quickly find that manually emailing people becomes a lot of work, and it is harder for people to stay aware of your events. Setting up some kind of online calendar system will reduce your effort in organizing events and allow you to focus on the next skill you want to learn to improve your club. For example, I started out just using a Facebook group for my calendar, but after about half a year decided I also wanted to start using MailChimp to provide weekly email announcements. This has added value to my club and increased attendance, but would have been overwhelming in the beginning had I tried to start with both.

Commit to new skills slowly to avoid biting off more than you can chew. There's a wealth of opportunity for places to go, things to do, and ways to organize your club. You don't need to start all at once. Everything takes time, so it is wise to commit to new skills slowly. When I first increased my events from two times per month to once every week, it was quite a bit of extra work. I also wanted to start doing some primitive skill-building events, but tackling both was just way too overwhelming, especially when it came to time. So instead, for the first couple of months of doing events once a week, I decided to repeat the best past events to allow me to focus purely on managing the more aggressive schedule. This worked well, and by the second month I was able to put some time into talking to naturalists and other folks to offer primitive skill building.

Grow slowly to ensure that you maintain stability. A lot of times, organizations will grow too fast—whether companies, events, or less structured groups. This can have very detrimental effects if you're not able to manage the growth effectively. In the case of a family nature club, as mentioned previously, the size of what you're managing is not just the number of members, but also the frequency of events and the complexity of those events. At the end of the day, focusing on the children's needs is a great barometer for guiding growth, and you'll find at the core that they need time in nature with a few friends. Great numbers are not required. Different places every time is not needed. It's time and space. Add to this gently and you'll be able to have a sustainable group.

Stay the course of your trajectory so that people understand what you are about and are able to plan their lives effectively. I've received a great amount of feedback from people saying that events every week works out very well for them because it is on their calendar now and it is just something they do every Sunday. Likewise, people "get" that our group is not about going on ski trips or doing hikes every week. I try to maintain a consistent direction in our events, and when there is an evolution coming I share that with the group in advance.

Jason's Picks

I launched with just a few friends and planned events that were very easy to scout, write up descriptions about, and participate in. As time went on, I started adding different kinds of events, such as boating and hiking, but I kept the group very small, including just friends. Next, I decided to add more people to the events, and once that was all running smoothly I decided to increase the number and diversity of events. It's been a wonderful process, and along the way I have been able to get good at skills I did not have mastered yet.

What You've Learned

In this chapter, you've learned how to start a family nature club, building one skill at a time.

CHAPTER 14

DISCOVER A WISE SAGE

A naturalist explains tree ring dating to my daughter. We estimated the tree was 95 years old!

9:53 AM. It is windy and chilly. Snow-capped mountains appear in the distance. We're geared up in coats, hats, and backpacks, and walking along a mountain trail with a naturalist. He selects a tree limb to use as a walking stick for the hike and explains the benefits of using walking sticks for locomotion, balance, and distribution of physical effort. We move along the trail like a group being guided through a museum, but in this museum you can touch and feel the things you see. Shortly we come to a stump alongside the trail. My daughter watches as the naturalist counts the rings and then proclaims the tree is older than she is, older than I am, and older than he is—estimated at 95 years old!

We continue on the hike. My daughter performs rock ballet. She gets dizzy and falls off the trail! She puts herself back together and bows. We trail run. We collect and smell sage. We collect quartz specimens. We look at beetle tracks on trees. During snack time there's a brief demonstration of how to sight using a compass. While we have been on this hike in the past, the added element of a naturalist provides a layer of depth to our environment and the flora and fauna that reside here. It becomes at once more magical and more concrete.

Imagine having the good fortune to discover a wise sage or elder that could guide you into nature. The stories of children who are accepted and made parts of tribes where they run barefoot across the wilds conjure visions of great and gentle knowledge and wisdom being transferred to a lucky individual. While there isn't exactly a surplus of wise sages waiting around to be discovered, you can very easily introduce educational and skill-building aspects to your family nature club.

How to Add Education and Skill Building to Your Events

Adding education and skill building to your events will vary a great deal depending on where you are located and kind of group you organize. There are a great number of options, whether your group is a private independent group, a public but independent group, a non-profit organization, or a group as part of a larger organization. In some cases, you can organize educational and skill building that is fee-based, and in other cases you can accomplish this freely.

Here are some ideas to get you started:

Public naturalist programs often exist on your city, county, state, and federal lands. Search the websites of these organizations to determine if they have programs offered for groups like yours. Frequently, you can work with these organizations to set up a special event for your group, or join an existing one.

Private programs are offered by a vast number of organizations working with children. In some cases, these may designed as paid programs that are not well suited for a family nature club. But often these organizations are flexible and open to setting up something unique for your group, and sometimes for nominal fees. Contact them to find out what kind of events could be designed, whether at their property or elsewhere. Organizations tend to develop their programs based on feedback from customers, so you should find an eagerness to collaborate on designing a custom program, if even as a way for that organization to better understand what customers want. As mentioned, there may be some flexibility with the price as well if it is understood that parents will be with their children, as that makes it easier for the program operator. When you contact them, explain your goals, introduce your group, and be up front about what kind of fees might be acceptable for the program you want to run.

Volunteer programs provide amazing opportunities for immersion that is otherwise difficult to obtain. Farms are a good example of this, where you can set up an event or find a farm with an existing volunteer day that you can join. Other existing volunteer programs can be found within public lands, such as forest projects for the county or animal habitat restoration (or animal counting!) at larger environments like those found at national parks. In these instances, you may find you can create an event that combines some volunteering, some education, and some play.

Jason's Picks

Now in my second year of organizing my family nature club, I am just starting to introduce educational and skill-building events, and I'm going slowly! I'm working on all three types of events, including working with the city naturalist program and talking to private program operators for primitive skill-building events, and have made a plan to take our group to a nearby farm this summer where we'll spend some time doing farm work and then have the rest of the time to explore the fields, play with the chickens, and muck about in the pond. I'm working hard to balance out these kinds of events with my other events so that we continue to spend a lot of unstructured time in nature and not add too much more learning on top of school.

What You've Learned

In this chapter, you've learned how to add educational and skill-building events to your family nature club by partnering up with other people and organizations.

CHAPTER 15

DELEGATE YOUR FEARS AND WORRIES

The children take turns with a hatchet and shovel, digging through the frozen surface of the ponds.

10:40 AM. We're out on frozen ponds in the middle of a winter wonderland. It's only 16 degrees but the children are dressed well and staying warm, passing a hatchet around and one by one taking swings at the ice. There are just over two dozen families (parents and children) at the family nature club, but even in those numbers watching children play with real tools in close quarters can be a bit unnerving. I'm happy to see that the adults in our group reinforce tool safety and stay engaged to ensure the rules are followed. The head of the hatchet smacks the ice and children lean in, quickly drawing instruction from parents to move back from the swinging of the blade. The hatchet is passed to the next child. More swings. More leaning in. More instruction to move back. And then . . . .

They break through the ice! Well, at least their hole is deep enough for . . . "Water!" "Water!" "Water!" "Water!" The hatchet is discarded and they scoop at the slush in the hole like this was an oasis in a desert. Eventually, we pack the hatchet away and run to other frozen ponds, exploring for hours in this winter wonderland.

Organizing family nature clubs can be confronting, scary, and overwhelming. Doing anything new is like this, and putting together outdoor events for children is no exception. Finding and participating in support networks will allow you to delegate your fears and worries to others so that you can be confident and stay motivated to build an incredible family nature club. While you may have yet to discover this subculture, there are a lot of other families and groups doing the same thing as you, and they can be of immense support in your journey.

How to Find and Network with Other Leaders of Family Nature Clubs

The level of support that you'll want for your family nature club depends on your experience and comfort level with what you're doing. In addition, who you will want to connect with will vary a great deal depending on whether you prefer in person or digital communications. In my experience, talking with others who have gone down the same path as you will make your process more efficient, surefooted, and profound.

Here's where to find leaders of family nature clubs:

Children & Nature Network is the organization founded by Richard Louv, author of *Last Child in the Woods*, the book in which family nature clubs were perhaps most popularized. The organization has done a great job of working to build an online community of leaders of family nature clubs, including producing a directory of the movement, which includes a map and contact list of leaders, organizations, and registered clubs. There is a specific list of contacts that can assist you in starting a family nature club in your area. Using the map, you can find existing clubs in your area.

Meetup is used by a large number of family nature clubs that you can find by searching keywords. Using your location as one of the search parameters will help you find active groups near you, including some that may not use the actual label of "family nature club," but that are structured and operate very much in the same way, under the same principles and purpose.

Google, Facebook, Instagram, and other social networks are also a great way to find people. Like searching on Meetup, you'll want to use specific keywords to help you find relevant groups. Explore the Web presence of the groups to determine if they meet your goals and would be good to connect with.

Building your own online presence by publishing and sharing content using relevant tags will naturally draw others into what you're doing. Talk about what you're doing, your challenges, your dreams, and your revelations, and people will find you and connect with you.

Attend local gatherings and events that resonate with you, or are being held by groups that resonate with you.

Once you find leaders that you want to connect with, there's a variety of ways to do so:

- Join their group and spend time introducing yourself so that people know who you are and what you are doing.

- Add value to their group by participating, and build relationships to ensure a future contact will be well received.

- Contact people directly and privately. In some cases, you can do this as a first step. In other cases, it's better to first get involved with their organization.

Jason's Picks

I began my journey getting familiar with the Children & Nature Network and connecting with leaders involved at that organization. As I became more confident in my group, I began to reach out to local organizers of similar groups and programs. More recently, I've begun building my online presence by sharing our adventures, which has resulted in like-minded leaders connecting with me. Everyone is very eager to help!

What You've Learned

In this chapter, you've learned how to network with other leaders of family nature clubs and similar organizations to get support as you build your own club.

AFTERWORD

Some of my earliest memories are of playing intently outdoors and simply being with the wonder of the natural world. Such experiences helped forge my deep personal relationship with nature, which has been the impetus behind my lasting academic and professional focus on the environment. In 2011, I began a doctoral program in which I researched the potential for family nature clubs to enhance social and ecological well-being. The purpose of family nature clubs, as articulated and promoted by the Children & Nature Network, is to gather children, families, friends, and community members together to enjoy nature on a regular basis.

Part of my research design was to create a new family nature club in my own community in central Maryland. I also worked closely with the Children & Nature Network to reach out to the leaders of family nature clubs and engage them, as well as the members of their clubs, in my study. In total, the results of my research weaved together insights from 47 family nature clubs, 348 unique individuals, and direct observations of 133 families that participated in outings with my family nature club, and my experience of designing, launching, and leading a new family nature club and participating in outings with my own family.

The key findings of my study cover multiple topics ranging from the amount of time family nature club participants spend in nature to their sense of connection with nature, sense of connection with their community, family-life satisfaction, social action, and household environmental behavior. Of particular relevance to this book, more than 20 distinct positive outcomes were identified for family nature club leaders and participants, both parents and children:

Learning opportunities:

1. Learning about places to go in nature

2. Learning about the natural world

3. Learning from leaders and/or other families (about ways to be in nature, ways to be with kids, etc.)

Nature connections:

4.   Spending more time in nature

5.   Developing a greater sense of connection with nature

6.   Increased environmental awareness and/or behavior

Family connections:

7.   Being more physically active as a family

8.   Having quality time together as a family

9.   Developing a greater sense of connection as a family

Social connections:

10.   Meeting new families/getting to know new people

11.   Developing a sense of community (friendships with like-minded people, etc.)

12.   Feeling a stronger overall sense of connection to the area we live in

Meaningful experiences:

13.   Had fun, memorable (interesting, exciting, adventurous, novel, etc.) experiences

14.   Experienced a sense of accomplishment and/or expansion of comfort zone

15. My child(ren) has enjoyed free play/playing with other kids (had the opportunity for independence, imagination, creativity, exploration, etc.)

Enhanced well-being:

16. Child(ren) having experiences that are positive for their behavior (problem solving, patience, sharing, independence, etc.)

17. Experiencing an enhanced sense of well-being (relaxation, joy, confidence, happiness, etc.)

18. Having experiences that foster a sense of connection to something bigger (spiritual, religious, etc.)

Reduced barriers to getting out in nature:

19. Fewer barriers to getting out in nature (more prepared, experienced, comfortable, and/or leveraging the planning done by the FNC leader, etc.)

20. A greater commitment to spending time in nature (setting time in schedule, getting gear such as play shoes that make it more viable, etc.)

Family nature club leaders also reported additional benefits, including enhanced personal relationships, increased well-being, a sense of personal accomplishment, increased leadership opportunities, and satisfaction from teaching people about and helping people to connect with nature. By all accounts, leading a family nature club is very enjoyable, gratifying, and well worth the effort. My personal experience resonates with these academic results. During the first two years of running my family nature club, I have had the great pleasure of watching children and adults gather together with focused excitement to look at animal tracks, examine beaver tooth marks, watch snakes slither into streams, touch a toad, cross creeks, and plant trees and gardens. The simple joy that came from sharing in these discoveries was contagious, and I am filled with hope that such experiences, replicated and expanded over time, will bring participants closer to each other and motivate their sustained care for the natural world. By offering a setting where families can regularly explore, learn, and grow together in nature, family nature clubs create a unique and very important opportunity for families to connect with one another, as well as their social and ecological communities.

This book clearly and compellingly presents the steps parents can take to start their own family nature clubs and bring these many benefits to their own families and communities.

Chiara D'Amore

Ph.D., founder of The Community Ecology Institute

http://www.communityecologyinstitute.org

CONCLUSION

In this book, you have learned a step-by-step approach to put into practice an evidence-based proven solution to help your children, your family, yourself, and your community unplug. There has never been a greater need in all of human history to focus on disconnecting from technology and reconnecting with nature. The steps are easy—you can start immediately with little to no cost, and at a scale that is comfortable and appealing to you. You have a wealth of resources available for you to make your effort easier, and a support community to help you along the way. You will find that creating a family nature club brings you immense joy, and results in profound, iconic, and quintessential childhood experiences for your children. Unplug and begin to reconnect today!

The End

JOIN THE COMMUNITY

If you haven't already, I'd love for you to join the Connect Your Kids to Nature community. You'll receive future books in the Connect Your Kids to Nature series for free when they release. You'll also get access to the free resources that accompany the books.

Unplugged Resources

Join my community and I'll send you a free handbook that includes easy-to-implement, research-based, and field-tested resources to help you start a family nature club. Contents of the handbook include:

- Benefits of Starting a Family Nature Club

- Family Nature Club Design Guide

- Outreach and Communications Strategies

- Event Planning Considerations

- Event Activity Suggestions

- Tips for Sustained Success

- Family Nature Club Planning Worksheet

- Family Nature Club Checklists

- Examples and Templates

- Additional Resources

For access to resources and join the community visit: www.jasonrunkelsperling.com/unplugged-resources

ABOUT THE AUTHOR

Getting your family outside for some EPIC fun is easier than you think! Are you ready to love being a parent again?

Parenting is like a marathon. No matter how much you know and learn, it's totally exhausting and overwhelming.

If you're struggling with mental and physical exhaustion from raising your children, you will be amazed at how quickly you can restore your balance when you get your kids into nature. Reclaim that precious time and rediscover how it feels to relax with a cup of tea so that you can fully embrace having a family.

Jason Runkel Sperling is dedicated to helping families get their children outside and into nature.

Before he discovered his passion for sharing his love of the outdoors with others, he struggled like many parents today with raising children in our modern times. During the first five years as a parent, Jason felt a deep and nagging anxiety. He was unhappy as a parent seeing his kids and their childhood consumed by screens. He took the plunge into raising his children screen-free and in nature because he knew he was the only one who could make the change he wanted to see in the world.

Since starting on this path, Jason has helped thousands of parents discover how to easily get their children outside and enjoying nature.

In 2013, his family moved from a one-bedroom condominium in Los Angeles to beautiful Boulder, Colorado, to create the childhood he dreamed for his kids. Thanks to an amazing community, supportive wife, and the Rocky Mountains, his children play with their friends in the bush, rivers, lakes, mountains, dirt, and snow.

Along the way, Jason made a lot of hard and expensive mistakes, and eventually learned the best way to give his family what they need. He wants to show you the way.

Jason's books are written to help parents like you find and master getting your children into nature, have more fun than you can imagine, improve your children's development, and strengthen your family—and all in the easiest way possible.

How are his books different? Pricey gadgets and programs are not required. In Jason's books, you'll discover for yourself that the most rewarding family experiences are straightforward and inexpensive. He'll show you how to get inspired and energized. Good planning is the path. The rest is a simple step-by-step process he teaches you.

More about Jason Runkel Sperling:

When it comes to helping parents quickly make meaningful and lasting changes in their children's consumption of nature, Jason walks the talk. He founded and has led Running Wild family nature club in Boulder, Colorado, since early 2015. He is a skilled and experienced outdoorsman who earned the rank of Eagle Scout as a youth, and went on to travel and live around the globe for 20 years, scuba diving, surfing, backpacking, skiing, rafting, adventuring, and completing a BFA and MBA. His bestselling books are to the point and action-oriented, and have reached thousands of parents, many who make life changes the very day they finish the books.

From mastering outdoor survival skills to leading groups of families into the wilds to sharing research on child development and cultural changes and navigating parenting a daughter and son with momma lion, his amazing wife, Jason loves the challenge of getting children off screens and into the great outdoors.

More at JasonRunkelSperling.com.

LIST OF IMAGES

Nyla and Silas in their best goofball pose as we're gathering gear for a family nature club event.

Introduction: Children sitting on tree at West side of Gross Reservoir, Roosevelt National Forest

ALSO BY JASON RUNKEL SPERLING

The Backyard Play Revolution

How to Engage Kids in Simple, Inexpensive Outdoor Play and Increase Child Health and Motor/Sensory Development

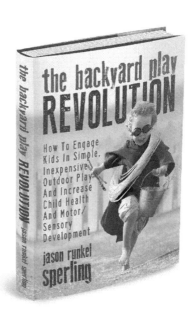

In this eye-opening, easy-to-follow, action-oriented book, Jason Runkel Sperling explains how to use screen-free, unstructured outdoor play and toys to increase early-age child learning opportunities and improve happiness for the whole family.

You'll learn:

- How to encourage your child to enjoy active, outdoor, screen-free play

- How to foster unstructured, child-led playtime

- The secret to making risky play work for your child

- Practical advice on how to pick the right toys and transform your backyard

- How to set up your backyard playspace and not break the bank

- And much, much more . . . .

Follow one father's entertaining and informative experiments to find play and toys that inspire his children to play outside, offline, and independently—like children of past generations. Author Jason Runkel Sperling shares his six-year journey discovering the history of play, playgrounds, toys, and the role of adults in their children's experiences, culminating in a revolutionary approach to backyard play. Full of humor, parenting insight, and in-depth research, Sperling's book will change how you think about raising children, and how you organize your home.

If you're like the majority of parents today, you may have noticed the differences in modern childhood. Unlike every other generation, your children spend more time indoors, glued to screens, and are less active and free to roam than in any time in history. You likely have come across countless articles on the epidemic of child obesity and behavioral problems today, and perhaps you've heard that getting children to play outside is an easy and inexpensive remedy. You may already want to get your children to play outside, but nothing seems to motivate them. Or maybe you're frozen with fear that they might get hurt if they go out. Plus, your backyard is manicured for adult enjoyment. So instead of heading outside, your children stay indoors, damaging their health and driving you up the walls.

You may have tried lawn games, sports equipment, remote control toys, or backyard arts and crafts, but nothing seems to hold their attention. And when you do spend time in the backyard, you always have to play with them. Or, perhaps you can't stand the thought of your children not getting ahead—so the children's schedule is jam-packed with adult-led, goal-based activities outside the home. In other words, you've turned into the family chauffeur.

Whatever happened to "go outside and play?"

Raising children today is harder than ever before, but children haven't changed all that much.

The best way to get children to develop their imagination and creativity, motor and sensory skills, emotional and social intelligence, and every other physical and mental ability, is to get them to "go outside and play" with open-ended, child-led play that can be enjoyed in the backyard. There are proven, evidence-based approaches for the role parents should take in facilitating this kind of play. And you can learn them quickly and apply them tomorrow.

This doesn't mean getting rid of every after-school activity, throwing away every toy in the house, or putting the kibosh on screen time forever. But it does mean making sure that children have the active playtime necessary to prevent physical and psychological maladies. It's vital, especially with early-age children, to give them the environment and support they need to develop. You don't have to play with children every second, you just need to know the right kind of play and toys to provide, and how to gently guide them.

The Backyard Play Revolution is for parents from every background, regardless of location or income level, and is appropriate for backyards of any size.

This book isn't hundreds of pages long. You can read it quickly and take action the next day. Are you ready to profoundly impact your child's life?

Get your copy of *The Backyard Revolution* at www.jasonrunkelsperling.com/the-backyard-play-revolution.

Mud Kitchen in a Day

How to quickly get your kids outside, playing in the dirt, & enjoying creative play

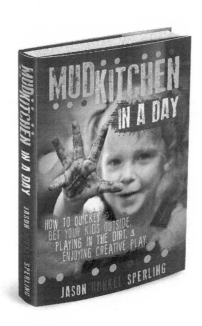

Looking for that perfect summer distraction to get the kids out into the backyard? Learn how to set up a simple and inexpensive children's mud kitchen in a day, allowing your children or grandchildren endless hours of plain and dirty backyard fun. Follow one father's entertaining and informative attempt to get his children outside, offline, and into the mud. Author Jason Runkel Sperling takes us inside his experience creating a backyard mud kitchen for his two small children. Full of humor, parenting insight, and in-depth research, Sperling's account will inspire you to create your own mud kitchen in a day, maximizing family fun, bonding, and creativity.

This easy-to-follow guide is appropriate for parents of any skill level and backyards of any size. Forgoing complex design, Sperling's mud kitchen guide focuses on the essential components of a mud kitchen using simple resources, allowing just about anyone to create a stellar children's mud kitchen in only one day.

Dozens of additional resources are included, such as:

- Where to get supplies, whether by making, finding, or buying them

- Outdoor play and its value to child development

- The value of dirt in building strong immune systems

- Comprehensive list of inspiring case studies, articles, and photographs of mud kitchens from around the world

Get your copy of *Mud Kitchen in a Day* now at www.jasonrunkelsperling.com/mud-kitchen-in-a-day

PLEASE HELP

If you enjoyed this book or received value from it in any way, then I'd like to ask you for a favor: Would you be kind enough to leave a review for this book on Amazon? It'd be greatly appreciated!

CONTACT

You can connect with Jason Runkel Sperling in the following ways:

www.jasonrunkelsperling.com

www.facebook.com/jason.sperling

www.instagram.com/jsperling

Made in the USA
Monee, IL
02 September 2023

42046178R00109